Twayne's United States Authors Series

EDITOR OF THIS VOLUME

Sylvia E. Bowman

Indiana University

Alexander Woollcott

TUSAS 305

Alexander Woollcott
in *The Man Who Came to Dinner*

ALEXANDER WOOLLCOTT

By WAYNE CHATTERTON

Boise State University

TWAYNE PUBLISHERS

A DIVISION OF G. K. HALL & CO., BOSTON

Library of Congress Cataloging in Publication Data

Chatterton, Wayne.
  Alexander Woollcott.

  (Twayne's United States authors series : TUSAS 305)
  Bibliography: p. 169–181
  Includes index.
  1.   Woollcott, Alexander, 1887–1943—Criticism and
interpretation.
PS3545.077Z64   818'.5'209   77-25123
ISBN 0-8057-7210-3

For Ardie
Who Dug Out
More
Than I Could Use

Contents

About the Author

A native of the Mountain West, Wayne Chatterton has earned a Normal School Diploma and Certificate from the Albion State Normal School, the B.S. and M.A. degrees in English Literature and Drama from Brigham Young University, and the Ph.D. in English Literature from the University of Utah. He has taught English literature and drama at Carbon Junior College, The Southern Idaho College of Education, and The College of Idaho. At present he is a professor of English at Boise State University.

In 1972, he originated the Western Writers Series at Boise State University and has served as co-editor of the series from its beginning. He wrote *Vardis Fisher: The Frontier and Regional Works*, which is the first booklet in the series. He is also co-author (with Martha Heasley Cox) of *Nelson Algren* in Twayne's United States Authors Series. He has just completed a *Monarch Notes* study guide on Nathanael West's *Day of the Locust* and a manuscript on Irvin S. Cobb for the Twayne series. For the next few years he will be at work on a two volume historical and analytical study of the novel of the Western Movement in America. These two volumes will be titled *The Novel of the American Frontier, 1780–1890* and *The Novel of the American West, 1890–1975*.

Professor Chatterton has served as a special lecturer in the American Studies Program at The College of Idaho, and he spent two summers as a guest instructor in the American novel and drama at the College of Idaho summer sessions which were conducted at Sun Valley. He was a Danforth Fellow in a seminar held at the Pacific School of Religion in Berkeley, California. He has also served as Idaho State Director to the National Council of Teachers of English and as Idaho State Chairman of the NCTE Achievement Awards.

Preface

A colleague of mine, a Jack London scholar at a California university, has just volunteered a confession that more than twenty years ago his reading of Woollcott's *While Rome Burns* inspired him to make some of his earliest experiments in the craft of writing. So he has shared a phantom ambition with the coterie of "intellectuals" who styled themselves the "wits" of my high school class in the late 1930s. Half a dozen of us were the "intelligentsia" in that small school in the Mountain West, and we considered ourselves very sophisticated. To a native New Yorker, we would have been yokels. Yet we knew about Alexander Woollcott. To us he was the highest ideal of wit and sophistication. We all wanted to write like Woollcott.

But the war came. Afterward, we had to finish college; and, in the meantime, Woollcott had died. There had been dozens of obituaries and widespread public eulogies, followed by the Samuel Hopkins Adams biography of Woollcott in 1945. Decades passed before the nation began to recall those early years in an access of nostalgia that reminds us that we have never quite forgotten Woollcott. Upon those of us who have loved literature and who have wanted to write, he has left his mark.

In recent years Edwin P. Hoyt has written his biography (1968), and Howard Teichmann has published his lively anecdotal biography of Woollcott (*Smart Aleck*, 1976) to serve as a companion piece to his highly successful "intimate portrait" of George S. Kaufman (1972). But until now there has been no single book length study of Alexander Woollcott as a critic and as a man of letters, nor even an attempt to provide a reasonably complete bibliography of writings by him and about him. In preparing this book, I have had the singular pleasure of rectifying these oversights.

One difficulty in writing about Woollcott as a literary figure is that only by way of dramatic criticism did he become an essayist, a *raconteur*, a verbal sketch artist, a master of the retold tale, a skilled artificer of general *colloquia*. For the first twenty years of his career, however crowded his life and however varied his literary experiments, he was foremost a drama critic. He held down his desk in one large newspaper office or another, he pursued the drama critic's hard routine, and he rode the critic's payroll. At least half of Woollcott's career, then, is a chronological series of events that attended his daily work as drama critic; but this period also included the various literary experiments that he made as a spinoff from his job as critic, and it culminated in his decision to become a full time, free-lance writer in 1928.

Thereafter he used his enormous energies to suit himself. The result was a bewildering variety of pieces for the major magazines. Eventually he also collected his favorite efforts to create his last two books, *While Rome Burns* (1934) and the posthumously published *Long, Long Ago* (1943). In this last major phase of his career as author, chronological events are of secondary importance; for, from a literary standpoint, it is more important to perceive his mastery of at least half a dozen closely related but separately definable literary types, most of which he labored hard to categorize in order to create some semblance of order in the two collections that gave him his stature as a literary figure.

In working out the plan for this book, I have tried to preserve the general lineaments of Woollcott's life and his literary career. The first four chapters, which are organized chronologically, begin with an overall survey in which I seek to demonstrate how thoroughly Woollcott's character and background have been absorbed into his work as author and critic. In Chapters 2, 3, and 4, in which I concentrate upon successive segments of his early career, I move in distinct phases from his early collegiate writings, his years as a cub reporter, and his stint as a war correspondent through his postwar career as drama critic. Here I have provided a detailed examination of each of the books that contain his collected reviews and essays upon the theater.

At this point, however, the chronological sections give way to three chapters that deal substantively with literary types and genres other than dramatic criticism. Chapter 5 deals with the three early books that most strongly demonstrate Woollcott's capacity for writing about famous personages with an adulation that amounts to hero worship; and coupled with these early attempts at book length composition is a discussion of Woollcott's two attempts at collaborating with George S. Kaufman in the writing of Broadway plays. In turn, Chapters 6 and 7 are devoted to summaries, analyses, and interpretations of four varieties of belles-lettres that Woollcott developed and refined during his later career as a free lance. These are his prolific and popular exercises in various kinds of trivia; his creation of what almost amounts to a twentieth century school of sensibility; his tendency to tell tales in the form of legends; and his unparalleled capacity to retell the most grisly murder stories in the tradition of the "merry murder," along with his passion for everything eerie and bizarre. Though his mastery of these forms had its roots in writing experiments that he conducted as far back as his college days, he reached the peak of his popularity and achieved distinction as a man of letters only after he had worked long as a free lance and had reprinted his own favorite selections in *While Rome Burns* and *Long, Long Ago*. Chapter 8 is an assessment of Woollcott's unique achievements as a critic and as a man of letters, but it also considers his contributions to the development of American literature and criticism in general.

I have provided detailed summaries and analyses of every book that Alexander Woollcott wrote or in which he compiled his own work. I have also provided judicious but generous discussions of and samplings from the drama columns that made him famous as a critic and reviewer. Though there are at present three substantial biographies of Woollcott, only Teichmann's contains a bibliography. Teichmann was interested almost exlusively in biographical material, however, and though his bibliography is invaluable for biographical information, it provides only minimal listings of other material. Therefore this book provides the first formally compiled Woollcott bibliography. By no means a complete listing, it does contain all important indexed material and many special items that should be of immense value to future Woollcott scholars.

Perceiving that a thorough presentation of all these matters has left no room for consideration of other interesting but less germane material, I have dealt only incidentally with Woollcott as actor, radio personality, letter writer, and arbiter of literary reputations. Though fascinating in themselves, these subjects are for the most part secondary to his career as man of letters. Nonetheless, I regret that I have been unable to make room for a chapter on Woollcott's letters. In the realm of private epistolary prose, there is nothing else like them.

In a critical study of this kind, the nature of Woollcott's writing creates unusual problems with documentation. Virtually all of his best work consists of extraordinarily short pieces. He tends to be nearest perfection in the highly polished literary sprint that uses between fifteen hundred and two thousand words. Therefore I have frequently found myself making repeated reference to a selection that covers only four to six pages and in which any really interested reader can find the references without serious inconvenience. In these instances I have been careful to locate the source clearly within the context of the discussion and have made all necessary references without the supererogation of end notes.

Until recently, Woollcott's books have been long out of print, but more and more of them are now being reprinted. I have used a handsome reprint edition of *Mrs. Fiske,* and within the past few years there have been reprints of the original Viking edition of Woollcott's letters and of the Viking Portable Library edition of his collected works.

WAYNE CHATTERTON

Boise State Universtiy

Acknowledgments

For valuable information that they have supplied by correspondence, I offer my gratitude to Nathaniel Benchley, Edwin P. Hoyt, Frank Sullivan, and E. B. White. I am particularly indebted also to Marc Connelly, that spry survivor of the old Algonquin Wits, who received me into the Park West apartment that he has occupied for over thirty years and who spent part of an afternoon in reviving memories of his old friend Aleck Woollcott. I am equally indebted to the late Arnold Gingrich, long-time editor and publisher of *Esquire*, who invited me to lunch with him at the Harvard Club in New York, where he told me a classic first person anecdote explaining why Woollcott was not represented in the first issue of *Esquire*, nor in any issue since that time. Though the anecdote has had no place in this manuscript, it was most revealing to one who has sought to understand all sides of Woollcott's temperament.

To the following librarians I extend my thanks for their willing and expert assistance: Darrel Huskey, Lois Cummings, Ione Jolley, and Cheryl Thompson of the Boise State University Library; Kathryn Mushake and Ardella Morrissey of the Idaho State Library; W. H. Bond and Carolyn Jakeman of the Houghton Library at Harvard University; Dr. Howard B. Gotlieb, chief of special collections at the Mugar Memorial Library of Boston University; and Walter Pilkington and Frank K. Lorenz at the Burke Library of Hamilton and Kirkland Colleges.

To William Shawn and Fred Keefe of the staff of *The New Yorker* I am indebted for their willingness to look through Woollcott's "Shouts and Murmurs" contributions in order to tell me the exact dates of Woollcott's earliest and latest contributions to that page.

To Howard Teichmann, whose Woollcott biography *Smart Aleck* (1976) was published while my manuscript was being edited, I am grateful for a long and pleasant conversation over the telephone. From the material in his biography I have gained some new information and have made some revaluations, most of which I have placed in the end notes. He is the only biographer of Woollcott who has provided a bibliography, and for biographical information his bibliography is at present the most useful.

By permission of the Harvard College Library I have used a short quotation from an unpublished letter of Alexander Woollcott to John (now Sir John) Gielgud, dated December 4, 1936.

For extensive use of quotations from Woollcott's drama columns, I am indebted to the New York *Times*. Specifically I acknowledge the use of material from the years © 1915/19/20/21/25/29/33/43 by the New York Times Company. Reprinted by permission.

As each chapter of this manuscript came from my typewriter, it was subjected to the scrutiny of my good friend and colleague James H. Maguire of the Department of English at Boise State University. For his perceptive criticism and his many practical suggestions I am most grateful.

I am particularly indebted to Dr. Sylvia E. Bowman for her thorough and expert editorial assistance in the preparation of the manuscript for this volume. After eighteen years in the post, she has given up the editorship of the Twayne Series. During that time she has meticulously read and edited more than five hundred manuscripts. Somehow, at the end of this remarkable career, she has found the time to give my manuscript the benefit of her vast editorial experience.

Aside from the dedication, I must also acknowledge an unpayable debt to my wife, Ardath, who is my research assistant, typist, and compiler of indexes. Let all shy and hidden facts beware. They are not safe from her.

Chronology

1887   Alexander Humphreys Woollcott born January 19, at Phalanx, New Jersey, to Walter and Francis Bucklin Woollcott, members of a cooperative Fourierist group.

1889– Moved with his family to Kansas City, where he spent his
1895   first years in public school. Returned to the Phalanx (1895), which remained "home" during a long period of family unrest while his father went from one job to another in widely separated parts of the country.

1895– Attended elementary schools, sometimes walking to ·and
1900   from the district school two miles from the Phalanx, sometimes living with the Agnew family in Germantown, Pennsylvania, in order to attend the Germantown Combined Grammar School. This period of unrest was so full of constant moving about that Woollcott's whereabouts at any given time is almost untraceable. The Phalanx was always "home" during summertime, however. Began keeping a diary and writing lavish reviews of professional plays, which he saw regularly.

1900– Attended Central High School in Philadelphia; boarded out
1904   while his mother and other members of the family lived at the Phalanx. Began his lifetime habit of voluminous correspondence. Wrote book reviews and essays for Philadelphia newspapers and continued regular attendance at professional theaters. Spent summers at the Phalanx.

1905– Attended Hamilton College near Clinton, New York; went to
1909   plays, participated in school dramatics, served as editor of the *Hamilton Literary Monthly*, twice won the college's "Ninety-one Manuscript Prize," sold a short story to a pulp magazine, and was graduated in 1909 with the degree of Bachelor of Philosophy. Suffered permanent damage from complications that left him impotent following an attack of mumps (1909).

1909– Took a position with the New York *Times*, first as reporter
1917   and then (in winter, 1914) as drama critic; fought legal battle with Shubert Brothers over the right of drama critics to make

adverse judgments of plays (1915).

1917 May: Enlisted for army service in the New York Post–Graduate Hospital Unit, with whom he served in France as Sergeant in Base Hospital No. 8; published *Mrs. Fiske—Her Views of Acting, Actors, and the Problems of the Stage.*

1918 Became member of the staff of the American Expeditionary Force weekly newspaper, *Stars and Stripes*, on which he served as reporter with Harold Ross and Franklin P. Adams.

1919– Returned to job as drama critic of the New York *Times;* pub-
1922 lished *The Command Is Forward*, a collection of stories from *Stars and Stripes.*

1922– Became drama critic for the New York *Herald*, where, with
1925 his colleagues Percy Hammond and Heywood Broun, he became known to theatrical people as one of the "Three Fat Fates of Broadway." Helped establish a residence club on Neshobe Island, Lake Bomoseen, Vermont. Published *Shouts and Murmurs* (1922), *Mr. Dickens Goes to the Play* (1922), and *Enchanted Aisles* (1924). Was awarded honorary degree of L.H.D. by Hamilton College (1924). Was transferred as drama critic to the New York *Sun* (1924).

1925– Became drama critic for the New York *World;* published *The*
1928 *Story of Irving Berlin* (1925); presided over the daily luncheons of the "Algonquin Wits," which included among its original and regular members Franklin P. Adams, Heywood Broun, Brock and Murdock Pemberton, George S. Kaufman, Marc Connelly, Deems Taylor, Robert Benchley, Dorothy Parker, Donald Ogden Stewart, Ring Lardner, and Harold Ross.

1928 Resigned from the *World* in order to travel and to write as a free lance; published *Going to Pieces* and *Two Gentlemen and a Lady.*

1929– Began weekly *New Yorker* column, "Shouts and Murmurs"
1930 (February 16, 1929), as well as a series of book talks in *McCalls*, titled originally "Reading and Writing" but later changed to "Dr. Woollcott Prescribes." Collaborated with George S. Kaufman in writing *The Channel Road*, a dramatic adaptation of de Maupassant's "Boule de Suife." Established a sustaining radio program called "The Town Crier," which he maintained intermittently through a national network and the British Broadcasting Company until 1942.

1931 Began his acting career in S.N. Behrman's *Brief Moment.*

1932 Traveled in Russia.

1933 Collaborated again with George S. Kaufman in writing the dramatic mystery-thriller *The Dark Tower.*

1934 Published his best-selling book, *While Rome Burns.* Concluded "Shouts and Murmurs" page in *The New Yorker* (December 29).

1935 Edited an anthology, *The Woollcott Reader;* continued to combine radio broadcasting with lecturing, especially at universities.

1936– Built and occupied permanent home on Neshobe Island,
1937 Lake Bomoseen, Vermont; edited *Woollcott's Second Reader* (1937).

1938 Acted in another Behrman play, *Wine of Choice.*

1939 Was the model for the characterization of Sheridan Whiteside, the central character in Kaufman and Hart's hit play, *The Man Who Came to Dinner.*

1940 Performed the role of Sheridan Whiteside in the West Coast Company of *The Man Who Came to Dinner* from January to April, when he suffered a severe heart attack, forcing the show to close.

1941 Returned to the road company of *The Man Who Came to Dinner,* but suffered a series of heart attacks after several broadcasts in England and a lecture tour in the Middle West.

1942 Recovered from heart attacks and continued radio broadcasts; began editing *As You Were,* a "portable library" for men in the armed forces.

1943 Died on the same night he suffered a heart attack while participating in the national radio program "The People's Forum" (January 23); burial urn placed in a grave at the Hamilton College cemetery, "the last dormitory" (July). *Long, Long Ago* published posthumously.

CHAPTER 1

Fabulous Monster:
His Life and Times

TO high school and college sophisticates all over America. Alexander Woollcott was an idol. To the aged and sentimental, he was a compassionate oracle. Yet, within a few years after his death in January 1943, his writings fell into obscurity.[1] Biographer Edwin P. Hoyt cites a single "remarkably simple" reason why the writer suffered so complete an erasure from public memory: that Woollcott's "most important work was done in the most transitory of media."[2] But this obstacle was only one of several that militated against the survival of Woollcott's hard-won literary reputation in the years immediately following his death.

Building his career by moving easily and constantly among the nation's best-known public figures, he became perhaps the most ubiquitous public figure of them all. As E. B. White has recently remarked, "Nothing Woollcott did or thought escaped notice. He saw to that."[3] And, as Woollcott waxed more and more the public figure, the public became less and less aware of him as a writer of smooth, engaging, and, in its own way, matchless prose. The irony is that, after his death, his literary reputation suffered most from a superabundance of that quality that is the essence of the familiar essay: the immediate and unmistakable presence of the author in the prose. So thoroughly had he become a Public Personality that, upon his departure, even his most devoted readers felt that his legacy of prose had somehow died with its creator.

Woollcott had, however, paved the way for his own neglect by refusing to consider himself a "literary" figure in any conventional sense. He despised the pedantic, and he scrupulously avoided dealing in profundities. Because he preferred to cast a new light upon a familiar tale, he had no interest in creating an original "classic."

19

Seeing no reason to expend his energies in a limited number of sublime flights, he deliberately contained himself within the range of invention that he recognized as his strength, and within that range he maintained his prolific and successful rate of production. As John Mason Brown declared "He was as untouched by sublimity as he was attracted by oddity."[4]

All these characteristics have been charged against Woollcott as weaknesses. Nobody has yet invoked in his behalf the Horatian dictum that a writer must know his limitations and must work within them. Though no writer of Woollcott's day had a larger number of true devotees, he was not fortunate enough to spawn posthumously a group of Woollcottian Janeites to defend his limitations as proof of his critical awareness rather than as his lack of talent. But in harnessing himself within his range, he overproduced. Responding to the ceaseless demands of a seemingly insatiable public, he saturated most of the popular media with the distinctive flavor of his prose. He appears to have spent his last years sustaining the interest of his readers through an unparalleled combination of person flair and sheer literary momentum, and this endeavor left his readers unconsciously jaded. At his death, they were psychologically released from what had become a kind of Woollcott habit.

Moreover, he could hardly have died at a historical moment more surely calculated by circumstance to insure his subsequent neglect. Of that generation that had most admired Woollcott and that might have been expected to perpetuate an interest in his writing, virtually all the young men were fighting in North Africa, in Italy, or in the South Pacific. At home, the "war effort" made almost exclusive claim to the public interest; and the enjoyment of belles-lettres had begun to seem unconstructive, vaguely useless, and even wasteful under the demands of national austerity. By the late 1940s, when there was once more leisure for such literary pursuits, Woollcott seemed somehow a part of another age and another time, though his writings were as contemporary as they had been during his lifetime. Even the biography of Woollcott by Samuel Hopkins Adams could not revive public interest in a writer telescoped out of memory by those few war years—despite the biographer's insistence that Woollcott was "anything but out of date."[5]

In the early pages of that biography, Adams recounts a "legend of suburban Philadelphia" that concerns Woollcott's response to a game at a children's party. The incident took place during that year of his childhood when he was, by his own description, "a nasty, sweet-faced boy of ten."[6] Along with the other children, he was invited to record his fondest ambition on a slip of paper. Shunning the usual childhood ambitions, he is said to have written, "I would rather be a Fabulous Monster."[7] The tenacity of this morsel of apocrypha is a token of the bizarre, startling, contradictory, and frequently domineering qualities in Woollcott's character and in much of his writing.

Perhaps the "fabulous monster" aspect of Woollcott's reputation was, as Frank Sullivan believes, no more than "a screen for a basic insecurity."[8] Perhaps it was mainly "a puton [*sic*], done for effect,"[9] as biographer Edwin P. Hoyt contends. Whatever its true nature, whether it was an alter ego or merely a mask, the "fabulous monster" of Woollcott's boyhood ambition became one of the most widely recognized aspects of his public image. It was the source of that flair for the outrageous that made his contemporaries inquire endlessly of each other, "What did Woollcott say or do today?"

I   *Child of the Phalanx*

Of the most important influences upon Woollcott's career, the earliest and the most pervasive, if also the most difficult to define, is the aura of independence and intellectualism with which the Fourierism of the Phalanx marked his character and his cast of thought. "The curious old Fourierist building, half barracks and half hotel"[10]—the eighty-five room house looming above the trees on the six hundred acre "domain" of the North American Phalanx in New Jersey—dominated Alexander Woollcott's childhood years even when the family was in Kansas City or in Germantown and following its restless father from one public utilities job to another.

During the lifetime of Alexander's maternal grandfather, John S. Bucklin, the North American Phalanx was one of several American experiments in communal living, and as a practical enterprise it outlasted the others including the much more famous Brook Farm project. The Phalanx was established in New Jersey in 1843 when a hundred and fifty staunch believers formed a colony that they planned to govern according to principles set forth in the writings of the eighteenth century social theoretician Charles Fourier. These principles were part of Fourier's universal formula for creating the best possible social enclave through the reorganization of existing societies into small social units. As Fourier had formulated them, all

social laws were to be derived from principles that governed the
physical laws of the universe. To Fourier, indeed, the universal
harmony that had to prevail in phalanx societies was supposed to
result automatically from a completely worked out mathematical
formula that Fourier spent most of his life in perfecting.

But the search for a definitive social application of the theory of
universal harmony was never resolved in the endlessly complex
writings of Fourier. Therefore, since the theory remains a somewhat
bizarre, appealing, but incomplete Utopian plan, Fourier's follow-
ers seize upon the most obvious of the social laws that he had
succeeded in developing. To avid advocates of Fourier, certain
ideals seemed revolutionary and practicable; and, when Fourierist
ideas came from France to America by way of the North American
Phalanx, his basic principles may have undergone a few modifica-
tions in order to justify their use in the American democratic society, but they remained recognizably Fourierist. At the time when
John S. Bucklin was president of the Phalanx, the members of the
community adhered to the Fourierist beliefs that each family must
occupy its own quarters in the common dwelling and that all members must share equally in profits from their common agricultural
and mercantile enterprises. The plan thereby emphasized the solidarity of the family unit and encouraged the keeping of private
property, even while it discouraged economic competition and obliterated social distinctions.

By the time Alexander Humphreys Woollcott was born into the
Bucklin family on January 19, 1887, the North American Phalanx
had largely disintegrated as an experimental social Utopia. But since
the Bucklins had inherited or otherwise acquired most of the
Phalanx property, members of the widespread family still occupied
the huge old Phalanstery building. In fact, fifty or sixty of Alexander's near and distant relatives by blood or marriage not only retained the Fourierist core of communal domesticity, but also supported other Fourierist beliefs that had prevailed among the original
colonists. Since several generations of Bucklins lived there "the
family" ranged all the way from the aged grandfather himself to an
indeterminate number of children, including several of Alexander's
cousins who were somewhat older than he. Indeed, the perennial
march to maturity of overlapping generations of Bucklin children
helps to account for the tenacity with which those at the Phalanstery
held onto educational theories that Fourier had considered indispensable to his social formula.

To modern educators, the most interesting characteristic of Fourier's educational theories is that they anticipate in many ways the "progressive" theories of teaching and learning that did not flourish in America until nearly a century after Fourier had first propounded them. Fourier taught that any useful form of education must be both integral and universal and that no distinction should be drawn between mental work and physical work. He demanded that the educational process be regarded as a form of play, and he insisted that subject matter be adapted to the interests of the learner rather than that the learner should adapt his interests to the subject matter. Consequently, an important aspect of Fourierist educational theory is the belief that younger children often learn best from their peers or from other children not much older and that, as part of their schooling, all children at an early age should be given responsibilities in the life of the community. Each child should accept responsibilities suited to his own interests. In the Fourierist scheme, these basic principles heavily emphasized the value of self-expression in all phases of the learning process.[11]

During Alexander Woollcott's childhood years, the Bucklins no longer held themselves solely responsible for the education of their young, as Phalanx families had done all the way through the school years of his parents' generation. Yet the Bucklins had no confidence that the public school system could instill in their offspring any of the Fourierist ideals for which they still retained a high regard. As a result of this dilemma, they had drifted into a compromise, and by means of the compromise, young Alexander was afforded a two-layered education, at least while he was in most of the grammar school grades. Complying with civic pressures that required for every child a period of formal education, the Bucklins sent their children to nearby public schools to get what the inhabitants of the Phalanx considered a commercialized schooling. But, for the sake of their own ideals, they also did everything possible to provide a basic Fourierist education within the family. As a result of this special homestyle education, Alexander Woollcott might legitimately be considered the first American writer to emerge from a system of "progressive education."

Being the youngest member of his immediate family, Aleck gained much from the family's adherence to Fourier's insistence upon the value of peer group instruction. His intellectual development was accelerated by the family's retention of a vestigial Fourierist familial organization, wherein aunts and uncles and

cousins assumed for themselves the various duties that each
member felt himself best qualified to perform. Because Aleck's intellectual precocity was his distinguishing characteristic among
members of his own generation, he received far more than the usual
share of attention from his Aunt Julie, who acted as governess for
most of the younger children. According to Fourierist dicta, he was
encouraged to pursue his own interests, especially in reading and in
artistic endeavors.

For Aleck, the Fourierist emphasis upon self-expression was of
singular importance, for the family placed a high value upon his
precocious experiments in writing and mimicry. Though his residence at the Phalanx was sporadic during those early years when his
immediate home was in Germantown or Philadelphia, he returned
to the Phalanx whenever he could; and he considered the Phalanx
his only real home from 1895 through his college years. His imaginative flights, his love of the theatrical, and even his growing eccen-
tricities met with the respect and the encouragement of his family;
but, in the public schools, these developments—including behavior
that obviously bespoke the origin of talent and originality—were
usually ridiculed.

Continuing to honor the basic Fourierist notion that all human
beings are born "with a complete set of interests, desires, and passions,"[12] the Bucklins of all ages lived in daily converse with literature and the arts. Those who possessed an innate love of literature
were offered every opportunity to know at least the standard classics
and to share their interests with other members of the family. Each
of those who loved literature was an advocate of one or more favorite
works, and it was a game among them to call each other frequently
by the names of fictional characters. So it was not merely a fay
impulse that prompted the Woollcott children to play the game of
quote-from-Dickens in order to announce the birth of Alexander.
With the Bucklins distraught at the arrival of another child in a too
large family, one of the children wrote and passed around a note
saying, "A young gentleman has arrived whose name is Mr.
Guppy."[13]

This mode of announcement, which might have seemed pretentious in an ordinary American household, was typical of the intellectual aura of the Phalanx; and so it is more than coincidence that
Aleck himself had a lifelong fondness for the novels of Dickens. His
high regard for Dickens, along with his fondness for other major

novelists, was largely the result of an intellectual heritage that his family took for granted. So strongly did he respond to intellectual stimulation that he cherished as little boy and young man the opportunity to learn under any auspices, public or private. A quarter of a century after he had first entered public schools, he credited his family background with instilling in him a "faith in the sheer magic of going to school."[14]

The artistic flair, the critical self-determination, the flamboyant idiosyncracies that were to mark his skyrocketing success as a writer and as a national figure appeared early in his life; but he later cultivated and dramatized the last of these as part of the public role he deliberately fashioned for himself. By no means a dull or boring child, he was bookish, highly imaginative, intensely curious, carefully selective of close friendships and private amusements; but he was not in the ordinary sense unsocial. Almost too refined of feature, he was considered a "pretty" child; and because his tastes frequently inclined him toward pursuits usually considered the province of young ladies, some of his public school classmates regarded him as unsuited for the usual roughhouse sports. Preferring croquet, he became so dedicated to that genteel competition that, during the height of his career, the croquet games that he generated upon the shoreward slopes of Neshobe Island became widely publicized as classics among the "backyard sports" of the nation.

II *Young Critic: Bookish and Bizarre*

The young Aleck Woollcott whose sensitivities flourished under the dotage of aunts and cousins was an Aleck (this is the way he habitually signed his early letters) to whom the outside world was sometimes less congenial; but it was that world—a world sometimes lonely and far from the Phalanx—that molded the public Woollcott.

He was only about two years old when his mother and all five of her children left the refuge of the Phalanx to join Walter Woollcott in a surprisingly metropolitan Kansas City, where the absentee father had landed a permanent-seeming position as secretary of the municipal Light and Coke Company. Little Aleck was to spend six years in this comparatively young and vigorous midwestern city. He was happy in the neighborhood friendships afforded by prosperous "Sash-Curtain Row." Moreover, he was lucky in his first associations with the professional worlds of journalism and the theater, and he was fortunate in the circumstances of his first years of public schooling. But he was depressed by a growing distaste for the irre-sponsibility of his cavalier father.

By the age of six, Aleck Woollcott had already decided that he wanted to become a journalist and drama critic. Both of these aspira-tions were suggested to him by his across the street neighbor "Rose" Field (brother of the famous Eugene), who took him to a spectacular performance of *Sinbad* and thereby gave him his first taste of the professional theater. At this performance, tantalized by stage illu-sions whose existence he had never before suspected, Aleck learned from "Rose" Field that drama critics received complimentary passes to the magic world of the theater. Two years later he had written a little tale, "The Adventures of a Shopping Bag," which "Rose" tried unsuccessfully to lodge in children's magazines. Nonetheless, unde-terred, the drama critic and man of belles-lettres had begun his career, sped along by his first stage role—as Puck in a neighborhood tableau.

In 1895, father Woollcott lost his job in Kansas City, and his wife and children returned to the Phalanx. From here Aleck walked four miles a day to attend the district school. As he read voraciously and comprehensively, he spewed forth an overstock of thoughts and inspirations in his newly discovered word-hoard. Sometimes during these years he lived with the Agnew family of Germantown near Philadelphia, and he found in George Smyser Agnew the only true chum he was ever to gain among boys of his own age. Young Agnew played a devoted Boswell to Aleck's juvenile Johnson, and these two precocious moppets attended the Germantown Combined Gram-mar School, where Aleck first adopted the eccentric and sometimes deliberately offensive behavior that his enemies were to fear from this time on.

Fully aware how different were his character and background from those of his classmates, he preserved his inner self by living mostly in that self rather than in the chaotic and uncongenial world outside. He kept a diary that began with the mention of Shake-speare and that contained regular notes upon his expenditures. At this time, he was not physically strong, but he was never inclined toward school athletics. In the external world, the bizarre and grotesque caught his attention. To these things he overreacted his-trionically and unleashed a mimic talent that could be vicious in its caricature. Since he was never afraid of larger or stronger boys, he was frequently beaten for his vicious imitations of their peculiarities.

For a time, living penuriously in a boarding house, he did oral readings before church and social groups and took roles in such club plays as Cox's *The Brownies in Fairyland*. Moreover, he haunted the galleries of the professional theater; and he entered into his diary criticisms of the current offerings. At this time he wrote mostly effusions upon the wondrous adventures of theatergoing. Later, as a celebrated critic, he refused to make a list of the ten plays he had most enjoyed, insisting that all ten would have to be plays he had seen as a schoolboy.[15]

III   *Fledgling Professional*

In 1899, after a stock market debâcle that shattered Father Woollcott's spirit and landed him in an institution, Aleck and Smyser Agnew entered Germantown's Central High School. Socially, Aleck was a misfit in this high school class, and he turned with increased energy to journalism and to the theater. Intellectually stimulated by the cultural and scholarly attainments of a well-qualified faculty, he established an independent school publication called *Silly Snippets*, where he published his own imitations of "Mr. Dooley." He also launched a similar publication called "The Garter," which he filled with satiric thrusts at his fellow students. Since he read almost incessantly, he borrowed two or three library cards at once so that he could load a small hand-drawn wagon with books at the local library every Saturday morning.

These high school years mark his entrance into the world of professional journalism. His receipt of a check for a book review he had sent to the Philadelphia *Record* was a spur to his ambition, and he was fortunate to have the special help of a distant relative, Miss Helen W. Sears, the book page editor of the Philadelphia *Telegraph*. Perceiving something unique in the bookish high school boy who sometimes felt free to pour over the fresh review copies in her workroom, Miss Sears proposed that he choose and keep any of the books he was willing to review for her. Moreover, she rigorously disciplined the immature and overwrought prose that he submitted. In a few months his reviews were good enough for him to be assigned the book page for a considerable time while Miss Sears was absent. At seventeen, he was already a working and successful literary reviewer.

Through all of his years at public school, however, the Phalanx remained the strongest and most pervasive influence upon Aleck's intellectual bent and temper. Wherever else he might have lived and studied temporarily during these years, the old Phalanstery building was the home of his heart and spirit. Not until he left for Hamilton College in 1905 was Aleck aware that he was irrevocably out in the great world. Then he was stricken with a nostalgia that never left him. At the height of his career he wrote an affecting little sketch about the "dear old house," saying, in his best sentimental manner, that it was "the one constant in the problem of a far-flung tribe."[16]

IV   *Hamilton College: Earliest Myth-Making*

Precisely why Aleck should have preserved so deep an affection for Hamilton College is not clear. These were the years when the almost undecipherable contradictions in his adult character first emerged. Furthermore, these were the first of his consciously myth-making years, and it has always been difficult to winnow the seemingly mythical Aleck from the real college student who worked and played and strove to achieve the goals that he had early and ambitiously marked for himself. Though this was a period of painful adjustment and self-cognizance, it was also just as undeniably one of the happiest and most usefully constructive phases of his life. He lived in restricted circumstances and was painfully aware that he was a "poor" boy among comparatively affluent companions. His public school lack of Greek forced him to work toward a lesser degree while duller graduates of private preparatory schools attained the higher degrees. He had to put up with more than his share of the collegiate and perversely affectionate epithets of "Putrid" and "Slimer" and to tolerate an excessive number of impromptu dunkings in the campus pool. But despite this disconcerting battery of adversities, the extraordinary boy from the Phalanx remembered those years with a sense of fulfillment and gratitude that made of Alexander Woollcott an almost worshipful alumnus and benefactor of the college.

As a budding critic and man of letters, Aleck found Hamilton College a priceless training ground. Having had some prodigiously early training in the *Record*'s routine reviewing and journalistic formulae, Aleck was ready to experiment with more highly imaginative and more purely "literary" forms of creativity. Of his interest in drama and the theater he was certain; but beyond this certainty lay the enticement of fiction, and everything in his background beckoned him in that direction. The elementary school pupil who had

taken home from the Germantown library small wagonloads of Mark
Twain, Louisa May Alcott, William Harrison Ainsworth, Charles
Reade, Charles Dickens, and Jane Austen was a boy who would try
his own hand at fiction when he was a college student.

During Aleck's last year at Hamilton, he met Samuel Hopkins
Adams on the campus, asked him for a recommendation, and invited him to look at files of "The Lit" as proof of his accomplishments as a writer and an editor. Although Adams was mildly offended by Aleck's seedy clothing and by the red fez with a gilt tassel
that Aleck wore in order to play the role of "Literary Aleck"[17] for
the benefit of the famous literary muckraker, Adams looked at the
samples of Aleck's writing; and his professional eye was impressed.

Having become editor of "The Lit" in his junior year, Aleck had
gone to work immediately to metamorphose the magazine from a
routine and unimaginative periodical into a lively and engaging
campus organ. Though some of his reader interest devices were
flagrantly obvious, they were also effective; and Adams perceived
that Aleck was possessed of innate editorial "flair." Moreover,
Adams was heartened to see that the quality of Aleck's editorials and
critical reviews was remarkably high. "The non-fiction contributions," Adams later confessed, "went far to obliterate the dire
memories of the Bohemian Nana and the virtuous Pearl."[18] (These
were names of overdrawn heroines in two of Aleck's short stories in
"The Lit.") Adams wrote guardedly to editor Carr Van Anda at the
New York *Times,* saying "It might be worth while to give him a
trial."[19] That recommendation was enough for Aleck. He did the
rest by himself.

V *Drama Critic versus Tradition*

Before he could get started on his career as journalist, he suffered
complications from a severe attack of mumps. At the time of the
original illness, he was working at a stopgap job as messenger with
the Chemical Bank of New York. Adams' letter had gained from Van
Anda a firm but courteous announcement that no opening would
occur until fall, and Aleck was doggedly renewing his *Times* application during his free moments, mostly on Saturdays. His persistence
impressed Van Anda so forcibly that, when an opening occurred,
Aleck went to work as a cub reporter in the city room; he performed
all the routine duties of the cub, and accomplished nothing spectacular for the first year or so. But he was learning the trade, and
learning it thoroughly. Toward the end of his life, he recalled that

during his first year he had written, among other routine assignments, dozens of colorless obituaries.[20]

Without flagrantly abusing the newsman's traditional regard for
the sovereignty of facts, he began looking first for the "slant"—for
the verbal tone or the fanciful cast or the coincidental sidelight or
the emotional charge that could give to an otherwise lusterless subject the flavor of originality and the appearance of significance beyond the facts. To other newsmen, Aleck's work as a reporter
seemed too "loose." But, after his first year as cub, he began to
move rapidly toward better and better assignments: from criminal
courts news to human interest stories, to rewriting, to general reporting, and at last to the position that he had sought and predicted
for himself since grade school days—drama critic.

When his opportunity came, it was a surprise to Woollcott, who
had overtly done nothing to place himself in line for the assignment;
but he had privately lavished most of his spare time upon the drama.
He had read everything he could find on the history of the American
theater as well as on contemporary theatrical affairs; and, despite his
meager salary as a cub reporter, he had been able to attend the
theaters as often as three and four times a week because the *Times*
routinely gave him unused free passes to current plays. Although
editor Van Anda knew little of Woollcott's special fitness for the job
nor of his lifelong desire to be a drama critic, he offered him the
vacant post because Woollcott had shown a flair for "dressing up" his
news stories and was capable of writing with style and originality.
Almost ecstatic, Woollcott accepted, and within a few weeks it was
clear to Van Anda that his choice had been appropriate beyond
every expectation.

By training and temperament, no man of that era was seemingly
better suited than Alexander Woollcott to spearhead the inevitable
clash between the independent *Times* and the critic-muffling theater owners and managers. Barred from the Shubert chain of theaters
for writing a mildly adverse review of *Taking Chances*, a badly
adapted French comedy, Woollcott relied upon the administrative
solidarity and the crusading spirit of the *Times* to see him through a
year long court battle that ended when the adverse publicity and
loss of theater patronage forced the Shuberts to renew their *Times*
advertising and to admit Woollcott once again into their theaters
without any restrictions upon what he or any other drama critic
could thereafter write about the plays. This confrontation dissolved

the traditional yoking of economics and criticism, for the purchase of high-priced advertising had carried the implicit understanding that a newspaper's critics would say only agreeable things about the plays. As a result of this important development in the status of dramatic reviewing, Woollcott became a force to be reckoned with.

VI   *Stars and Stripes: War as Drama*

When the war fever spread across America in 1917, Woollcott had already written and seen into press his first book—his conversations with the famous actress Mrs. Fiske, which gave some solidity to his reputation as a literary man. But the qualities that kept him abreast of his time, or even ahead of it, were his crusading spirit and his driving desire to be always where the "action" was.

Leaving his column in the hands of Brock Pemberton, who later passed it to John Corbin, Aleck joined a medical unit, Base Hospital No. 8, and spent several months in a camp near the Breton village of Savenay. He spent much of his off-duty time at Mère Cocaud's *buvette* in the village, and he frequently had visits from friends, especially from Heywood and Ruth Hale Broun, who were on journalistic assignment in Paris. Though he avoided military drill and other rulebook obligations that he regarded as useless, he performed his assignments well enough to be made a sergeant, a military rank beyond which he had no aspirations. He also put together a play, which was well received by his unit and by others nearby. In February of 1918, a wire from the Surgeon General requested that Sergeant Woollcott be sent to Paris for duty with the newly established army newspaper, *Stars and Stripes.*

Once again he had brought with him just the right combination of gift and training to make the most of the unexpected opportunity. His stories (though unsigned) were among the most widely read in an army publication that eventually reached wider circulation than that of the *New York Times.* After the war, moreover, the founding and guiding spirits of the now world famous Algonquin Round Table were, besides Woollcott and Heywood Broun, several of Aleck's close friends and co-workers on *The Stars and Stripes.* Most notable among these were Franklin P. Adams (F. P. A.), whose widely read column "The Conning Tower" became the main public record for the "Algonquin Wits," and Harold Ross, founder and editor of *The New Yorker.* There was also John T. Winterich, journalistic chronicler and anthologist, whose reputation as a copy man was unsur-

passed. Aiding these capable journalists on the production side of
The Stars and Stripes were the original editor, Guy T. Visknisski;
Seth Bailey; Hudson R. Hawley; and two particularly talented art-
ists, C. LeRoy Baldridge and A. A. Wallgren.

As a field correspondent, Aleck reached the front in May 1918 and
began sending back to Paris a steady succession of stories based
upon firsthand reports, front line general knowledge, and direct
observation. To the former New York drama critic, these battlefields
were the most dramatic spectacle on earth; and his stirring vi-
gnettes, profiles, panoramas, and small sagas reminded even the
most bitterly disillusioned soldier of the valorous ideals with which
America had entered the conflict. The battling foot soldier, feeling
lost save as a pawn in a vast, impersonal game of dying, responded
to Woollcott's vision of him as the unsung hero that every man felt
himself capable of being. The thousands of unrequited deeds
seemed more meaningful as part of a manifest destiny unperceived
on the battlefields when they were reported in Woollcott's despatches.
A dedicated front line soldier, if a most unsoldierly one, Aleck himself became more and more famous as the baggy, wide-eyed, be-
spectacled, ubiquitous Med-Sergeant correspondent who appeared
in A. A. Wallgren's popular cartoons.

Through the hardships and dangers that Aleck had deliberately
sought in pursuit of his material, he had honed his writing edge on
the hard and brittle carborundum of life at its most desperate and
fundamental. During the long period of demobilization, he was able
to look back upon it all, to search out its meaning for a peacetime
world, and to develop the "mature style"[21] that characterized his
best work thereafter. With all its horrors, the war had been kind to
Aleck.

VII *Postwar Times: Seidlitz Powder Stylist*

Back home, Aleck resumed his place on the *Times* and began
writing for the magazines, at first desultorily and mostly in order to
pay some debts. He rode out the Actors' Equity strike of 1919
without alienating good friends and without being traitorous to
loyalties on either side. Since his own prewar victory over the
Shuberts had made it possible for the drama critic to exercise his
true judgment, to exert influence upon taste in writing, acting, and
production, Woollcott wrote his reviews to give his readers an accurate description of the plays they might want to attend. Since no

other critic in New York was better suited to perform this function, Aleck was soon "the most courted and best hated critic in the business."[22]

The whole postwar world of letters, arts, and journalism was undergoing rapid changes; and the tendency of journalism to merge with, or at least overlap, the field of arts and letters was one of the most radical changes of all. Consequently, Woollcott and his fellow critics were now legitimate practitioners in a distinct literary genre. Book reviewing and its allied journalistic forms, too, were no longer an incidental service and had become a function of general interest news. This tendency toward the literary found willing and highly competent advocates in such widely read columnists and critics as F. P. A., Christopher Morley, Don Marquis, George Jean Nathan, Percy Hammond, and Woollcott.

When Woollcott emerged in the early 1920s as a leading literary figure among New York journalists and critics, one of the singular forces that propelled him into literary notice was his aptitude for turning to his own advantage what others considered as adversities. The writer who provided him with the earliest occasion for exercising this aptitude was George Jean Nathan, whose sophisticated waspishness created the opportunity. The occasion was one of Nathan's *Smart Set* articles, titled "The Seidlitz Powder in Times Square."[23] Nathan opened this diatribe with an ingenious if somewhat strained broadside against the *Times* drama department in general; then, switching his focus to the new *Times* critic, he viciously challenged Woollcott's qualifications and his competence to judge matters theatrical, scoffed at Woollcott's unbridled enthusiasms for leading actors and actresses of the day, and ridiculed his style.

But, because the excess of Nathan's diatribe went beyond the worst excesses that he intended to charge against Woollcott, the general effect of Nathan's article was to arouse sympathy for Woollcott and to heighten interest in Woollcott's criticism. Few things could have publicized Woollcott's writing more widely or more effectively; for, despite Nathan's intent to annihilate Woollcott, he unwittingly provided instead a lively description of Woollcott's style. The reading public knew by now, even if it had not known before, that whatever else Woollcott's writing might be, it was most assuredly lively, colorful, and above all engaging.

From this time to his death, Woollcott was never out of the public eye, either as a writer or as the multifaceted "public institution"[24] that he had become by 1936. Immediately after the "Seidlitz Powder" incident, he refused lucrative offers from night clubs, as well as suggestions that he take his highly saleable talents to Hollywood. Despite the fact that his first two books, *Mrs. Fiske* and *The Command Is Forward,* had created no particular excitement in the book trade, he chose to spend the summer months of 1921 at Hamilton writing books. Here he finished his manuscript of *Mr. Dickens Goes to the Play* and a collection of his Sunday essays on the theater titled *Shouts and Murmurs,* both of which were published in 1922.

Returned to the *Times* in the autumn, working with young George S. Kaufman as his assistant, Woollcott continued writing for the magazines. He amplified his reputation as a critic and increased his already comfortable market value as a writer. At the same time, he expanded his exotic circle of friends and acquaintances, which included a few marvelous eccentrics and shoals of celebrities from every field of endeavor. From this point, his career falls into three perceptible divisions: the *Herald* years from 1922–1925, the *World* years from 1925–1928, and the free-lance years from 1928 until his death.

VIII   *The* Herald *Years*

Nothing was to demonstrate so clearly the high market value of Woollcott's work as Frank Munsey's offering him the position of first string drama critic on the *Herald* at the top flight salary of two thousand dollars a month. With this turn of events in October 1922, he became what he was to remain for the rest of his career—one of the highest paid critics and authors in America.

The mid-1920s were Woollcott's peak years as drama critic, and they were also the years in which he fully established his wide circle of close and influential friends. During this time, too, he had virtually preempted the now famous Neshobe Island house as a residence club for himself and for the friends he wished to entertain. Besides being awarded the honorary degree of Doctor of Humane Letters from Hamilton in 1924, he managed to publish more books than he did during any other similar length of time in his career: *Mr. Dickens Goes to the Play* and *Shouts and Murmurs* in 1922, *Enchanted Aisles* in 1924, and *The Story of Irving Berlin* in 1925. This increase in literary production was partly the result of his astute demand that the *Herald* allow him four months of each year to pursue independent writing and editing.

Woollcott's years on the *Herald* were also the ones when the original "Algonquin Round Table" was bursting into national eminence. Woollcott, one of its founders, was one of its most prominent figures throughout its existence. According to the account of Frank Case, proprietor of the Algonquin Hotel, "The Round Table lasted longer than any other unorganized gathering that I know of. It began in 1918 when Woollcott came home from the War and it continued without a break and with almost no change in the cast for more than ten years."[25] In 1922, the daily Algonquin luncheon was a nationally recognized gathering of New York's most brilliant personalities. Unique of its kind in America, this group gradually attracted a larger and larger circle of international celebrities and was to "burgeon in an atmosphere of intellectual stimulus, wisecracks, and no-limit poker, and to endure through more than a decade as a landmark of highbrow rubberneckery."[26]

IX   *The* World *Years*

By 1924, the struggling young journalists, dramatists, humorists, and critics of the Algonquin formative years had waxed famous, each in his own right. As a result, the luncheon gatherings, originally spontaneous and sprightly, had become an ongoing public spectacle, and the badinage was self-conscious and often painful in its effects. However disagreeable the daily display of wit may have become for many of the Round Tablers, it remained the ideal vehicle for the public Woollcott.

In the era of the "wisecrack," to which the Round Table gave style and impetus, Woollcott was an acknowledged grand master of the art. "Woollcott," says Corey Ford, "was high priest of the Cult of Rudeness, perfected at the Round Table—the Vicious Circle, the group called themselves—where abuse was the accepted form of conversation; and his extraordinary vocabulary made his insults cut like a surgeon's scalpel."[27] Woollcott, a gifted writer, was also a consummate showman.

During a few months in 1924 and 1925, he served reluctantly as drama critic for the New York *Sun,* Munsey's afternoon newspaper, to which he had been transferred when the *Herald* was sold to the *Tribune.* The reassignment to an afternoon paper seriously disrupted Woollcott's lifestyle, including his writing habits. But at the expiration of the Munsey contract, Herbert Bayard Swope, executive editor of the *World* and a close acquaintance of Woollcott, offered him a contract of fifteen thousand dollars a year, a thirteen week annual vacation, and permission to spend his spare time writing magazine articles. Pleased with the special sanction to write independently, Woollcott accepted the position.

For nearly three years, until the spring of 1928, Woollcott remained as drama critic for the *World*. He was stimulated by the company of F. P. A., Heywood Broun, Lawrence Stallings, Deems Taylor, Harry Hansen, H. L. Mencken, Ring Lardner, and Frank Sullivan, but he was also harried by the too close supervision of Swope and by Swope's daily barrage of memos. Woollcott's circle of friends—mostly celebrities, but also enlivening eccentrics who caused Dorothy Parker to describe him as "a connoisseur of goofy specimens"[28]—had become so large and so important to him that he needed more time to devote to their cultivation and entertainment. Moreover, he so fully occupied himself with preparing material for the magazines that Swope had begun to complain.

By this time, Woollcott had done some harrowing and some objective self-assessment. His conclusions concerning his own strengths and weaknesses as an author suggest that he had an acute capacity for self-criticism. Reducing his conclusions to their rudiments, he had decided that, beyond his proved accomplishments as drama critic, he could expect to excel only as "gossip, wit, raconteur."[29] He had reason to believe that, within these limitations, narrow as they might be, no writer in America could equal or surpass him.

X   *The Ubiquitous Free Lance*

Woollcott left the *World* at the expiration of his contract in the spring of 1928. If Swope had lost patience with his drama critic's heavy moonlighting in the magazine field, he so regretted the loss of his star performer that he offered him an extra thousand dollars to stay. But Aleck refused. Though newspapering had been good to him, he was tired of the routine. He was tired of Swope's oppressive supervision, and he was frustrated by a range too narrow for the full exercise of his talents. He chafed under the time pressures that prevented his producing the fully developed, mature, colorful copy he wanted to write.

The risks of free lancing did not worry him. He felt free to live for short periods of time in the South of France, and he traveled to England, Japan, China, Russia. Offers from magazines jostled each other to reach him; he had more invitations for lecture tours than he could accept; his name and face were so well known that he was beset with, and accepted, opulent offers to do testimonials for Muriel cigars and Seagram's whiskey. Moreover, the baby-giant radio industry soon persuaded him to do the "Town Crier" program, which he broadcast on a combined nationwide and British network from 1929 to 1942. This regular broadcast, along with the national radio program "The Early Bookworm," brought his voice into most American homes. By means of radio he became more than a national institution; he was a household personality.

Free from the strictures of newspapering, he turned his energies to a staggering variety of artistic, literary, and critical enterprises besides radio. Still enthusiastic about the theater, and feeling a proprietary interest in it, he twice collaborated with George S. Kaufman in writing plays, and three times he attempted acting roles. Neither of the plays he wrote with Kaufman was a real success: *The Channel Road* (1929), an adaptation of de Maupassant, lasted for only fifty performances; and *The Dark Tower* (1933), a melodramatic treatment of murder as comedy, was instantly panned off the stage by the critics. As an actor, he accepted roles apparently tailored for him in two plays by S. N. Behrman. The first of these was *Brief Moment* (1931), in which he was so perfectly typecast that he kept the play going for 129 performances, largely by getting all possible mileage out of what he called "an actor-proof part which fits me better than any suit I ever had did."[30] The second of these plays was *Wine of Choice* (1938), in which, after personally revising Behrman's dialogue for smoother delivery, he played the role of a wise-cracking Jewish cosmopolite who meddled in the careers of young people. *Wine of Choice* ran for three months on the road but for less than half that time in New York.

In 1939, responding to a rather casual suggestion by Woollcott, George Kaufman and Moss Hart began work upon a comedy that deliberately and brilliantly satirized the almost mythical aspects of Woollcott's life and career. Woollcott himself worked enthusiastically as an informal adviser to the collaborators; for, far from being incensed at the overblown portrait of him that emerged in the character of Sheridan Whiteside, he did everything he could to make *The Man Who Came to Dinner* a success. From as far back in his career as the "Seidlitz Powder" diatribe of George Jean Nathan, Woollcott had realized that he would profit rather than suffer from any caricature of his public image.

In the first few lines of the play,[31] all of Sheridan Whiteside's speeches are unmistakable variations upon the vituperous verbal thrusts that Woollcott habitually made as the recognized master of the high art of insult. Whiteside's entrance line—"I think I may vomit"—is an example of the raw language that Woollcott frequently used for its shock effect, especially when he was in society that was generally considered "polite." When Whiteside addresses his secretary as "Repulsive," he uses the very term that Woollcott habitually employed in addressing his familiars—but, paradoxically, only in addressing those whom he truly liked. Moreover, Whiteside's high-handed commandeering of a private home and his manipulation of people's lives are fully consistent with the behavior of Woollcott, who had become famous for assuming proprietary rights over the lives of everybody who came within his sphere.[32] At the beginning of Act Two, when only a week has passed since Whiteside took over the Stanley household, the untidy abandon of the room is typical of Woollcott's famous apartments in which fast-paced living, the holding of daily levees with famous people or bizarre characters, and almost ceaseless work were indistinguishable functions of his lifestyle.

For the purposes of dramatic characterization, all these aspects of the character of Sheridan Whiteside are merely adaptations of the well-known "fabulous monster" attributes of Alexander Woollcott. But the fascination of the play, as well as much of the reason for its continued success, lies in the subtle and believable way in which the stage character of Sheridan Whiteside achieves a blending of the contradictory elements in the real life character of Alexander Woollcott. By the end of the play, the character of Whiteside transcends the superficial and overly obvious image of a mere egomaniac who tramples indiscriminately upon all who get into his way. Somehow, as a result of Whiteside's monumental nastiness and his insufferable high-handedness, all the other people in the play get whatever they deserve in the way of reward or punishment. The literary effort of a fatuous small town doctor is properly ignored, a grasping and devious sex siren is carted away to Nova Scotia in a mummy case instead of getting a choice part in a new play, and the moral veneer of an ultrarespectable small town family is peeled away by Whiteside's brilliant discovery that the closely harbored sister of Mr. Stanley is an infamous ax murderer. This discovery, which would otherwise seem far-fetched, is a believable result of Whiteside's authority as a student of bizarre murder cases, just as Woollcott was.

On the other hand, the way is also paved for Whiteside's secretary to marry the young man she loves, and two young people are freed from the shackles of overprotective parenthood. In the unravelling of these events, Sheridan Whiteside exhibits all the warmth, the enthusiasm, the loyalty, the perception, the generosity, and even the unexpected kindness and sentimentality which, as with Woollcott, lay carefully concealed under the disguise of a "fabulous monster." The triumph of the play lies in the capacity of its authors to dramatize the character of a real man so effectively that audiences have not had to recognize the actual counterpart of Sheridan Whiteside in order to appreciate the comedy, however much that appreciation may have been heightened for those spectators who also knew about Woollcott. The fact that the character of a real person could be so successfully used is also a unique triumph for Alexander Woollcott, whose real life role playing was capable of being transferred almost literally to a fictional role in one of America's best-known plays.

With Monty Woolley and Clifton Webb as Sheridan Whiteside in concurrent productions of *The Man Who Came to Dinner*, the play was an instant hit, and a long-lived one. For a short while, Woollcott himself performed the part in the West Coast production, but much of the time he was plagued by illness. The play has enjoyed revivals on the stage and in movies, and it was especially adapted for national television production as late as the 1970s.

From the time Woollcott left the *World*—in the same year when he published his last collection of exclusively theatrical criticism, *Going to Pieces,* and his widely read troika of dog stories, *Two Gentlemen and a Lady*—he continued to write apace for the magazines. To publishers, his name was magic, a "Midas touch."[33] Offering top rates, editors would outbid each other for his material. He established for himself strict work schedules and bombarded the magazines with every kind of story, sketch, retold tale, reconstructed crime, reminiscence, interview, anecdote, folklore, fantasy, and high coincidence episode that his comprehensive mind and his unflagging memory could compound.

At some point early in this period, Woollcott managed to switch his immense influence as drama critic to the world of letters. His gift, observed Harrison Smith, "lay in some mysterious emotional affinity with the mind of the ordinary man which was not apparent to those who knew his peppery and irascible nature."[34] By microphone and magazine he charted the fortunes of popular writers of the era. His lone but insistent voice frequently raised unnoticed or neglected books to the status of best sellers and long-lived favorites.

In the late 1920s, he had established a durable series of book reviews in *McCall's*. At first titled simply "Reading and Writing," but changed to "Dr. Woollcott Prescribes" after the critic had received the honorary degree from Hamilton, this series had already become the platform from which he delivered Olympian fiats upon the value of literary work. In 1935 and again in 1937, he extended this function to selecting and editing wide-ranging materials from other writers. Using this material, he made two curiously eclectic anthologies. *The Woollcott Reader* and *The Second Woollcott Reader*, both of which openly mirror Woollcott's personal enthusiasms. Both collections were highly controversial, especially among scholars and other critics; but both were widely read. At the time of his death, he had prepared the equally wide-ranging but somewhat more conventional selection *As You Were*, one intended as a "portable library" for the armed forces of World War II. Later, Viking Press adopted Woollcott's subtitle as the general title for its highly respected series of anthologies.

Woollcott twice plundered the nooks and crannies created by his own hundreds of contributions to various periodicals and selected his own favorites to bind into book form. Surely there is not in the history of American letters a more curious and intriguing mélange of twice- and thrice-told belletristic exercises than *While Rome Burns* (1934) and *Long, Long Ago* (1943). The first is by all odds Woollcott's most successful book and the one considered typical of his best work.

Demands upon his time had become incredibly heavy; his social life, complex. He resorted to scheduling everything tightly for months ahead to prevent his multifarious nonliterary activities from interfering with his writing. He began seeing friends and conducting business in his apartment while he answered his mail and even while he dictated articles to his secretary. In 1936, he purchased a considerable portion of Neshobe Island, built a stone house near the residence club that he had leased for years, made the house the center of his pursuits, and installed himself as a lavish but absolute despot over an intellectual mini-kingdom of his own. In some of

America's most brilliant social, artistic, and intellectual circles, the highest accolade was an invitation to spend some time at Neshobe Island with Woollcott. Novelists and playwrights went there to pursue their current writing projects. The activities on the island, notably the no boundary croquet games, rapidly became legendary, as did the madcap antics of Woollcott's close friend Harpo Marx.[35]

But the pace of such living took its toll. Fond of rich and exotic cuisine, Woollcott considered his regular indulgence in gourmet foods an essential part of the good life he had made for himself. In this regard, as in every other, he refused to consider the consequences, one of which was an immensity of corpulence far beyond the effects of the "beastly complication" of his childhood illness. By 1934, he began to have trouble with his circulation and was forced to lose fifty-five pounds by dieting. But thereafter he continued his indulgences until the spring of 1940 when he was in San Francisco playing the role of Sheridan Whiteside in the West Coast production of *The Man Who Came to Dinner*. Succumbing to the famous restaurants of that city, he overate and suffered a severe heart attack. Early in January 1943, while appearing as a guest commentator on a radio network program, "The People's Forum," he suffered a fatal heart attack.

With the interment of his ashes in the cemetery at Hamilton, the "Woollcott legend" became one of the perennial puzzles in American arts and letters. Woollcott's lifelong capacity for evoking violently opposite reactions in people gave rise to a widespread game of "Who was the real Alexander Woollcott?" His character was by no means neatly integrated, and as a result he appeared a different person to different people. It is not surprising that Frank Sullivan can say "in the years I knew him, and knew him well, I never found him a 'monster,' "[36] but that another close acquaintance can say with equal sincerity "I want nothing to do with Woollcott, dead or alive."[37]

Those who have striven most objectively to discover the essence of his character have depicted him in terms of those contradictions that were themselves his character. These contradictions forced George S. Kaufman to select "IMPROBABLE" as the only single word in the English language that adequately describes Woollcott. Samuel Hopkins Adams resorts to the device of compounding separate ingredients in the hope that, together, they will suggest the nature of the whole man: "To Mr. Pickwick's rotundity add a pinch of Sheridan Whiteside's waspish temper and a dash of Bernard Shaw's diabolic wit. Lace plentifully with the milk of human kindness, add a cupful of treacle and you have the recipe for Alexander Woollcott."[38] In a similar fashion, John Mason Brown constructs a tissue of fractious references and mixed metaphors: "He was not only a man of contradictions; he was an anthology of antitheses. He was a tantalizing mixture of those two Nicks—the Saint and the Old; a baffling combination of tomahawk and treacle, of adder's nest and bon-bon box. Was he a scorpion? Well, he could also be an overdose of saccharine."[39]

Only such a man could have written in so distinctive a tone and style upon such a variety of matters, but critics tend to speak of his writing much as they speak of the man. This tendency is especially true of those who, like Booth Tarkington, were themselves literary figures of considerable reputation: "the focus of his admiration might be a book, a play, a painting, a philanthropy, a college, or an orphan child, or an octogenarian lady or a fugitive Colonel or a miraculous dog or a Vermont cook or an eloquent scientist."[40] But no matter how kaleidoscopic the nature of Woollcott's interests or of his manner of writing about them, there is general agreement that he approached every writing task in the same spirit: "His secret— though he made no mystery of it; indeed, he spent his days trying to convey it to the world at large—was his extraordinary rapture with life."[41]

With good reason the president of the board of editors of *The Saturday Review of Literature* seized the occasion of Woollcott's death to warn that "the future literary historian of our time will find himself mentally tortured when he reaches this extraordinary man."[42] Even so, one conclusion seems clear: both the man and his work share the qualities that made him one of the best-liked writers of his era. Marc Connelly declares of Woollcott's work after thirty years of retrospect, "some of it is memorable, perhaps not imperishable."[43] Yet Woollcott's writing is never dull, nor has it ever been accused of being so.

CHAPTER 2

The Woollcott Way

BECAUSE Alexander Woollcott could hardly remember a time when literary concerns had not been central to his intellectual and emotional life, and because he had learned so early the value of his private perceptions, his writing developed into "the perfect thermos bottle for his likes and dislikes."[1] This is not to say, however, that Woollcott was always instinctively right about the nature of his own talent; for in his formative years, he was especially susceptible to popular literary and artistic fads. By any of these he might have been lured into that limbo of lost artists who beat their wings endlessly in darkness, unable to find their way back from premature sorties into uncongenial regions of their art. Instead, though Woollcott sometimes experimented with standard literary forms, he never allowed himself to become immobilized by the need to "prove himself" in pursuits that were manifestly uncongenial to his talents. As a schoolboy, he had an eminently practical sense in these matters. By relying upon this sense, he learned something useful from each experiment: he moved forward even in his failures. The most obvious example of this pragmatic sense is his concerted attempt to create fiction during his college years.

I The Hamilton "Lit": Prizes and Projections

From his first weeks in college, Woollcott bombarded the pages of the *Hamilton Literary Magazine* with short stories that were direct reflections of his current reading and other personal interests. Though Aleck was precociously independent in most other creative and intellectual matters, in the writing of fiction he seemed unable to rely upon inspiration beyond the most stilted and artificial of popular models. These were probably the literary models most popular among Aleck's classmates, for "The Lit" was full of experiments similar to his.

All of Aleck's contributions to "The Lit" are carefully preserved in the periodical files of the library at Hamilton and Kirkland Colleges. The general reaction among those who have investigated them is that Aleck was fortunate to get fiction writing out of his system as early as he did, for his performance in this medium was irremediably sorry. But if these stories are read in the proper perspective, they are not quite so deplorable nor so uninteresting as they have been made to seem. In the steady succession of Aleck's contributions to "The Lit," for instance, there is a cluster of short fictional narratives that are early experiments in the sentimental, the bizarre, the grotesque, the exotic, and the coincidental. They are, in fact, experiments in the kinds of writing that eventually became Woollcott's special contribution to American belles-lettres.

"The Hearth and the Cloister"[2] is a sentimental story in the "little orphan girl" tradition. In this tale, a small orphan girl puts up such a spirited rebellion against the inhumane authoritarianism of a smug Mother Superior that the middle-aged Mrs. Blake undergoes an unexpected maternal resurgence and takes the little girl into her own home. As in all Aleck's stories of this type, the dialogue is stilted; the diction, stereotyped; the situation, too patently contrived. Woollcott, one must remember, was at the age when even the most worldly young man is likely to be most callow: he was a college freshman who was trying to deal convincingly with a most sophisticated situation and with mature emotions far beyond his years. But, because he saw himself as a rebel, he deeply sympathized with the little girl's rebellion against unjust authority; and in these scenes his story is at its best.

Aleck continued to pour out stories with a regularity that hinted at the developing professional; and in June 1906, "The Lit" announced that "The '91 Manuscript Prize has been awarded to the story entitled 'The Precipice,' by A. H. Woollcott, '09." Aleck's story, which had appeared in the February issue,[3] was the first story to win the literary prize that had just been established by two Hamilton graduates of 1891, Samuel Hopkins Adams and George M. Weaver, Jr. Subtitled "A Story of Bohemia," "The Precipice" is an exotic tale of temptation, debauchery, and sudden regeneration that draws upon all the moral dissolution with which the word "bohemianism" had become charged in the years immediately following the turn of the twentieth century. In the story, Nana (whether with Zola's heroine in mind, Woollcott has never confessed), whose fresh and "unconventional" charm has captivated all the jaded hearts among the bohemian studios, is ready to pursue the wicked allurements of this unfettered life. She is on the very rim of a moral precipice when a messenger brings from her uncle a package containing a picture of her dead mother, a picture of a face very much like Nana's. But because "the great grey eyes looked at her reproachfully, accusingly," Nana perceives with revulsion that "the fair lights of Bohemia were calcium; the gayeties tinsel; the beauties tawdry." As Nana hears Bonny's footsteps approaching, she flees. "Just in time, mother," she whispered, "just in time."

Whatever its excesses, the story afforded Aleck an exercise in the piling up of effects and in the use of what he conceived to be the sly and brilliant repartee of the sophisticated world. This repartee includes a reference to Camille, along with some erudite but painfully lascivious classical banter by Nana: "I never heard of lady and gentlemen vestals. . . . I'm afraid the great fire would have gone out." Moreover, for the first time in his career Aleck made one of the multiple sales for which he became a wonder of the publishing world. After he had received the prize money for "The Precipice," he sold the story for twelve dollars to the pulp periodical *The Bohemian.*[4] He had parlayed the original twenty-five dollar prize into thirty-seven dollars—a considerable sum in those days, especially for a college student who had to wear his summer clothing all winter.

Like most students captivated by Classical studies, Aleck frequently mistook erudition for creative talent, and sometimes he could not keep pretentious erudition out of his fiction. In "An Old Dodge, or the Wisdom of Solomon,"[5] he produced a satiric parable-anecdote in which, at a great trial in Hades, Solomon must settle once for all whether Bacon or Shakespeare had written the great plays. Judge Jeffries, Blackstone, and Mrs. Siddons ("musing tragically") agree that the wise one seems "up a stump," but Solomon resorts to an "old dodge" that has worked before. He declares that, because the claims of Bacon and Shakespeare balance equally, the great works shall be divided equally between them, the dividing to be performed by Augustin Daly "with shears and blue pencil." But, when one of the claimants pleads that all the plays should go to his opponent rather than that the precious works should be mutilated, the case is thereby decided in favor of the one who demurs. For Aleck, the little tale is an exercise in Swiftian and Popean satire; but

it is also an early display of the literary and theatrical name dropping
that he later raised to a form of high art in the informal essay.

In general, he perceptibly gained judgment and control as he
went on laboring with fiction through his college years. "Paradise
Lost, Being the Story of Another Eden"[6] is also a tale that involves a
sophistication, maturity, and worldliness beyond Aleck's years and
personal experience; but even so, it cannot be charged with the
blatant sentimentality of "The Hearth and the Cloister," with the
exotic excesses of "The Precipice," with the affected erudition of
"An Old Dodge," or with the facile superficiality common to all
these stories. Better focused and better controlled, it is the story of
a powerful love between a handsome young artist and a beautiful
woman whose bouts with the surgeon's knife have made it impossible for her to "be a wife to any man."

Nevertheless, he pledges his life to her, and she replies, "All my
life, I will do all I can to make you happy," a remark that becomes
the key refrain in the narrative. Unmarried, they brave social ostra-
cism to occupy together a house in a small college community,
where Craig can paint while she devotes herself to making him
happy. But he is soon possessed by a strange restlessness; she, in
turn, by a nagging apprehension; but both reactions are dissipated
for a time by Craig's absorption in painting a long-planned portrait
of a peasant girl, employing as a model a sweet-faced local girl of
seventeen. Seeing in the nearly finished portrait "a living thing of
passion," Esther realizes that she herself "seemed a thing of lovely
marble, but marble and the girl in the painting was flesh and blood."
Stealing unnoticed upon Craig and his young model one hot afternoon in a willow grove, she finds them kissing. Not knowing that it
is their first impulsive embrace, she silently retreats to the house
while Craig is shocked into awareness by his model's unwitting echo
of Esther's words, "I will do all I can to make you happy." Rushing
in true penitence to Esther, he discovers her dead in a chair facing
the window, with the evening light glinting upon the barrel of a
revolver.

If, in his enthusiasms, the virile and sophisticated hero of this
story sometimes talks like a Hamilton College senior, still the subtle
and yet often profound emotional conflicts of the heroine are more
convincing than might be expected of a fictional character drawn by
a writer who was himself only a college senior. In this short-lived
period of experiment in fiction, Aleck was usually most convincing

in the creation of female characters. There seemed to be little question that "Paradise Lost" was good enough to warrant the '91 prize for this year, and that the characterization of Esther was a sufficient advance over that of the bohemian Nana to lend greater respectability to the prize itself.

Among Aleck's attempts at fiction are, of course, a few of the usual college boy stories about college life. "Pearl"[7] is a slight narrative about "Billy" Drexel's infatuation with the new waitress who serves Billy's college clique at Colby's restaurant. Just before he asks her for a date, he is saved from a foolish mistake by the disclosure that she is married and has a baby. Billy's infatuation with Pearl is largely the result of what Aleck apparently considered her brilliant repartee. She charmingly squelches the irresistible Crenshaw[8] by replying to his query as to whether she is called Pearl because she is without price, "Oh no, . . . It's because I am cast before swine." This is, of course, the kind of devastating badinage with which Aleck himself later destroyed those whom he suspected of presumptive afflatus. He produces a somewhat more substantial but still a thin and immature college story in "The Rushing of Timothy Starr."[9] In this story, a blasé and self-centered college senior, Rexford Gay, makes an altruistic gesture toward a lost and disillusioned freshman who is ready to leave for home. As a result, the worthy freshman is taken into the fold, and Gay thereby redeems himself from being "the most damnably selfish man in the crowd."

A few of Aleck's Hamilton "Lit" stories are set in the theatrical world that was always his abiding interest. In these stories he did the best he could to project himself into situations that he conceived as typical of the world of Broadway playwrights, players, and critics; and, though nothing in his experience at this age could have given him the insight necessary to an adequate understanding of the arcane and tragic professional mysteries of "The Swan Song,"[10] he created scenes that were an augury of his own future. He did the best he could to create the atmosphere of the "characteristic New York first night," which he was to experience and even to help create as one of the leading critics who "would be there in full force," and even as a "banished critic" like his fictional Estabrook. He tried to reproduce the jaded scepticism of the critics and their lofty exchange of predictions. He tried to capture the rarified surprise of these critics upon seeing "acting as no one ever acted before."

The "Swan Song" of the tale is the final performance of the New York stage star Constance Dean, who, on the opening night of a role that most critics feel is far beyond her powers, discloses to her leading man that, though she is on the verge of long-expected heart failure, her performance will be her final declaration of a love for him that she could not reveal until this moment. Her performance is awesome beyond anything ever seen on Broadway, but she dies at the end of the second act.

Similarly, "The Hand of the Potter"[11] contains Aleck's vision of the cynical, self-seeking inconstancy of the theatrical world and its hangers on, wherein genius is often fraudulent and fame is fickle. Like the lady in the opening paragraph, Aleck was later to be accused of "being something of a connaisseur [sic] in notables"; and, of all the most formidable New York critics of his time, he was to be the best-known chronicler of just such vagaries of theatrical reputation as that in which Hilda Satterlee begins by being known as "the wife" of a famous playwright but ends as the true celebrity who relegates her basically untalented mate to his deserved place as merely "the husband."

As keenly as Aleck must have felt the compulsion to test his powers in imaginative literature, he continued to supply "The Lit" with book reviews and with informal essays upon the theater. Not surprisingly, considering his previous training by Miss Sears of the *Ledger*, these critical essays show him at his best during his college years. In these works he anticipates the conversational ease and sureness, the eye for illuminating trivia, the fascination with biographical detail, the perception of paradox, and the propensity for wide-ranging comparative judgment out of which he later wrought his distinctive tone and style.

In his first months at Hamilton he produced a historically based book review in which he employed the comparative method that most college freshman find awkward and complex but that Aleck in "Two Novels: A Comparison"[12] uses with ease and naturalness. He achieves unity and coherence without strain; he presents his conclusions with unforced assurance. He points out that, though the straightforward candor of Malet's *Sir Richard Calmady* resulted in the expurgation of offensive passages from that novel, the veiled immorality of the Baroness von Hutten's *Pam* has allowed that book to be accepted and widely read. His conclusion follows from the pertinent query whether taste in literature is commonly regarded as more important than ethics: "Indeed, it would seem so. We must, before all else, be perfectly and precisely proper."

"Richard Mansfield"[13] is one of the first in a long succession of informal essays, profiles, personalized musings, and critical commentaries that reveal Woollcott's intimacy with the American theater. Even as early as his college years, Aleck had somehow discovered the "trick" of beginning with a proverb, anecdote, quotation, or general reference which appears impossibly remote from his real subject, but which, by imperceptible twists of viewpoint, leads the reader into the true subject with deceptive leisureliness and with unsuspected relevance. In this essay, he prefaces the context with one of Bernard Shaw's remarks concerning the making of heroes, and his opening paragraph uses the prefatory quotation as a springboard for some interesting speculations upon "our tendency to overdo things in general and particularly when it comes to lavishing praise on the last man to die." From here, he moves subtly to the recognition that the recent death of the eminent actor Richard Mansfield, like that of Joseph Jefferson, was marked by a surprisingly guarded response in the articles and editorials in which one would expect him to receive approbation commensurate with his professional stature.

To explain and at the same time to remedy this unwarranted neglect, Aleck provides a remarkably thorough and equable consideration of the positive and negative values in Mansfield's personality and professional attitudes, of the comparative strengths and weaknesses in his most famous stage portrayals, and of the possibility that a living actor like E. H. Sothern or David Warfield might be able to fill Mansfield's now vacant place in the American theater. Aleck's conclusion is that Mansfield's niche "seems destined to remain empty." All in all, this early essay in theatrical criticism reveals a surprisingly advanced grasp of theater history and a mature sensitivity about the distinctive contributions of its leading figures. Here and there Aleck shows himself capable of making the kind of sweeping but perceptive observation by which he was to become so highly influential as a dramatic critic, as when he thus explains the perpetual tendency to neglect even the most eminent of deceased actors and actresses: "there is something in the very nature of the profession that they followed, which is ephemeral and leaves nothing but a memory to spur our enthusiasm."

By commencement time, Aleck could see that the continued belaboring of fiction would not be worth the candle. It seemed clear that his strength lay in the freshness of his observations, in his viewpoints and opinions themselves, not in the contrivance of imagined character and incident, wherein he seemed unable to do more than mimic current fads or outworn traditions. However disappointed he was to discover that he could not hope to excel in the literary mode of Reade and Dickens that he so much admired, he turned again wholeheartedly to his undiminished dream of being a drama critic. The single pursuit of this goal meant, of course, becoming first a competent professional journalist, and he persisted in referring in later life to his first years on the *Times* as learning his "trade."

He never wrote short stories again, and he refused to attempt the writing of novels at all.[14] But his early experiments with fiction were by no means lost. His fascination with imaginative writing which remained with him all his life, colored, heightened, and intensified his presentation of factual matters. As a result, his future writing had a singular fusion of emotional involvement and play of fancy that was uniquely Woollcott's. If fiction was not his forte, still few other writers in America could so smoothly and so ingeniously treat fact as though it were fiction.

II *The Woollcottian Essay*

At some point during his apprenticeship as a writer, Woollcott realized that his own *propre persona* was far more fascinating than any fictional or dramatic character he could invent. For one who had been forced to accept the bitter probability that he could not excel in imaginative writing, this discovery had wide-ranging implications. Since the reading public found him so captivating, he could serve as the hero of whatever he wrote. In a multitude of different ways, in virtually all of the nonfictional forms, he could speak directly to his readers, could share with them his inmost affections, could bombard them with his likes and dislikes, could even, like any true familiar, offer them advice. For these reasons, Woollcott's whole career is substantially an ongoing autobiography—partly confessional, partly gossip, partly personal crusade, partly spleen venting, partly secret sharing, partly self-projected bedtime story.

In his positive selfhood resides the continuing modernity of Alexander Woollcott. Long preceding the successive generations of beatniks and hippies, all in their own way bent upon discovering their selfhood and "doing their own thing" in a world growing more and more depersonalized, Woollcott proclaimed and celebrated his indefatigable individualism with every sentence he wrote. He was fortunate that the familiar essay had reached a phase in its development that cried out for a specialized twentieth century counterpart of the great individualist essayists of the past—for a "personality" writer who could endow the essay of the 1920s and 1930s with at least a suggestion of the "flavor" that Sir Richard Steele, Oliver Goldsmith, Charles Lamb, and Washington Irving had been able to bring to the "periodical" essay of the eighteenth and nineteenth centuries.

For, as a literary genre, the familiar essay of the early twentieth century had been deprived of much of its traditional savor by a tendency to confuse it with a product of the prevailing periodical press—the "article." The leisureliness, the whimsy, and the reverie that readers had expected of the older essay had given way to a twentieth century demand for varieties of informative or persuasive writing. Sheer authorial charisma and stylistic felicity were less important than content; therefore, the typical reader of the twentieth century "article" was unaware that he was reading a derivative of the "essay" at all. This loss of grace and urbanity tended to produce a singularly pedestrian literary form; and among the writers of "specialized essays," "special features," "columns," "profiles," and other kinds of "articles," serious and talented writers like Heywood Broun and Woollcott continued the older traditions in guises appropriate to twentieth century tastes. Woollcott managed to combine some of the best features of the familiar essay and the article, thereby gaining a massive reading public, most of whom were happily unaware that he was giving them a high order of personal essay, costumed as "articles."

In his popular pieces, Woollcott met his readers on their own ground. He possessed an uncanny sense of what would appeal to his readers, partly because he shared their tastes and interests. Though his curiosities were more intense than theirs, his interests broader, his powers of discernment superior, his peculiar affinity with the mind and the heart of the common reader is still one of the remarkable phenomena of our literature. "To a very large extent," Charles Angoff wrote several months after Woollcott died, "he was the quintessence of the public, feeling its every lowly emotion, dreading its every dread, sharing its every exultation, and following its every tear with one and sometimes two of his own."[15]

To supply the content—the informative base—that current taste required of the article, Woollcott had only to consult the rich catalogue of his own interests and experience. By way of Woollcott's prose, the bored or harried or fancy-starved American citizen of the Jazz Age and the Depression era could pursue his own closest and most secret enthrallments: the private lives and public behavior of celebrities; spectacular rises from poverty to success; sensational crimes; bizarre coincidences; heroic actions; heart-warming sentiment. Most surprising of all, though the "common man" of the time looked upon professional book reviewers as elitist cognoscenti with offensive academic pretensions, he trusted and welcomed Woollcott's effusive recommendations for good reading. He was even willing to let Woollcott give him public lessons in grammar and composition.

The clue to Woollcott's mysterious rapport with American readers lay in the capacity of his prose to evoke a companionable sense of sharing. This sense is, in turn, the device by which Woollcott bridged the gap between the apparently outdated familiar essay and the article. In the latter, the tone is usually objective, and the relationship between author and reader is an undemanding neutrality. More than any of his contemporaries, Woollcott conveys the impression that he is standing at the reader's elbow, sharing experiences with a friend or acquaintance whose interests are very much like his own. Therefore his readers, whatever their social class or level of education, were led to feel that he was one of their own; and, because "he insisted upon making every hour an adventure in friendship and originality,"[16] they found his enthusiasms, indeed his every least vagary of mind and heart, infectious. This quality of his prose is Woollcott's unique contribution to American literature.

In American literature, Woollcott may have been the earliest literary counterpart of the popular idol. Masses of people were interested in what he thought and said, just as they were becoming infatuated with the private lives of movie stars and other popular artists of the entertainment world. Sensing that his wide readership was much like a live audience, Woollcott realized also that in many ways each of his literary pieces was a form of public performance. As a result, he wrote in the familiar tones of the raconteur, and he sustained his literary performances by wreaking endless variations upon the device of the first person singular, especially in his opening sentences, where he quickly established the personal tone of voice that would prevail throughout the piece. "Let me begin by admitting . . ." he would say, or "When I read in the cabled obituaries . . . ," or, as in his reports from abroad, "I am just back from Leningrad." As in "Gift Suggestion" from the "Book Markers" section of *Long, Long Ago,* where he refers to himself as "one who is still an enthusiast for the old custom . . . ," he often spoke familiarly in terms of his own attributes, and he evoked sentiment by frequent reference to "these old eyes."

Over and over again he used such openings as "Once upon a time . . ." and "This is the story . . . ." Perfectly aware that scholars condemned these openings as trite and taboo in respectable story telling, he knew also that his own readers loved him for his lack of literary pretension. The tone of these openings is the familiar tone of the fairy tale and the oral story, and among children these forms of story telling have almost universal appeal. One of Woollcott's best professional secrets was his knowledge that his adult audience wanted him to write for them in the old familiar tone of the children's story.

The Woollcottian essay itself tends to be intimately conversational in tone, prolifically anecdotal in method, and basically analogical in structure. A highly familiar tone and the liberal use of anecdote have always been common elements in the personal essay, but Woollcott created unique variation of the type by using elaborate forms of the anecdote as a basis for analogies, which serve in turn as the basic structure of the essays. If not all of his essays employ this characteristic blend of combined narrative and expository elements, his most popular and successful essays have been those in which the combination has worked best, just as his least successful ones are those in which the combination has failed to work well.

Typically, the Woollcottian essay moves by the carefully contrived appearance of indirection or even by the appearance of misdirection. When the method works well, the reader is startled but not offended to discover that the charming, leisurely, engaging, and usually trivial matter in the opening paragraphs is not the real subject of the essay at all, but only a parallel of the true subject. By a form of analogy, the true subject appears to crop up almost accidentally. Frequently the relationship between the opening tale and the main subject is so remote that the reader's surprise at discovering the main subject becomes almost superseded by his recognition that Woollcott's linking of the two is a form of literary prestidigitation. The technique is a difficult one, and precarious, requiring of the

writer unusual finesse in the use of proportion, emphasis, and timing. Woollcott's triumph is that the material in the opening paragraphs or pages—however trivial or seemingly inconsequential—is
just as entertaining and effective as the main subject, if not more so.
In his own way, Woollcott shares with his idol Dickens the capacity
for making the most of amusing sidelights.

For any critic or raconteur, however, and for Woollcott in particular, the danger in creating the analogic essay lies in the temptation to make more of these anecdotal analogues than of the dominant
idea. From time to time, Woollcott becomes lost in his exuberances,
and the resultant essay suffers from bad proportion and misplaced
emphasis, as in the essay on Pauline Lord.[17] Here Woollcott attempts to glorify the London debut of Pauline Lord by comparing its
reception with the French enthusiasm for the Second Division
doughboys who marched in the Fourth of July parade in Paris in
1922. More than half of the essay is Woollcott's emotional account of
the parade and of his own patriotic pleasure in perceiving "that
every Frenchman in that tossing multitude was thinking: 'Here is
the real thing from America at last.' "

By the time he reaches his main subject, he is himself uneasily
aware that his initial enthusiasm is disproportionate to his purpose,
and he remarks, "All of which may seem a journey around Robin
Hood's barn" in order to introduce Pauline Lord's performance in
Anna Christie at the Star Theater in London. The long introductory
account is too obviously a journey around the barn—so much a
journey as to overshadow his assertion that "if it had been my portion to be in the stalls that night . . . I should have felt the same
emotion which strangled me that July morning in Paris five years
before. There certainly was the real thing from America at last."

As Woollcott realizes, but is apparently powerless to remedy, the
emphasis in this essay is divided and the proportion overbalanced in
favor of his initial enthusiasm. It is difficult for a reader to know
whether the real subject is the popularity of the American
doughboys in France during the war, the London success of Pauline
Lord in the Eugene O'Neill play, or American patriotism in general.
But, in the Woollcottian essay, proportion cannot always be measured by a foot ruler. Often it is more accurately measurable by the
weight or intensity of the content, or by timing, or by placement.
When the basic analogy is felicitous, Woollcott is likely to play with
the elements of his essay, as do virtuosos in all of the arts. At these
moments, he may attempt any structural experiment that seems

peculiarly suitable to his subject, however untraditional or bizarre the experiment might seem.

In "The Corporal of St.-Aignan,"[18] for instance, he devotes fully three-quarters of the essay to a leisurely discussion of living conditions in Russia (as he saw them during his Russian trip of 1932); and he warns his American readers that, "when you hear that some Russians live on the fat of the land while others are in want, it is important to keep in mind just how lean the fat of the land is at this difficult stage." Hereupon, with not more than a quarter of the essay left to write, he remarks in a seemingly off-handed but obvious interpolation "—one gets to the point at last—." The "point," as he presents it to his reader, is the anecdote that involves the corporal at St.-Aignan whom he had mentioned briefly in his first paragraph as a person who came more often to his mind during his Russian tour than had Stalin, Lenin, or Marx. The anecdote, slight and humorous, concerns the experience of one Sgt. Clutterbuck, who, after leaving the "sink-hole" camp at St.-Aignan to spend a luxurious year in Paris, returns to find the corporal still living in the mud at St.-Aignan. When Clutterbuck asks indignantly whether he had been "stuck here all this time," the corporal replies, "Why, I'm sitting on the world. Got a wood floor in my tent and everything."

At first, the essay seems badly out of proportion. But it works well enough because Woollcott has pulled a "stunt" on the reader by declaring that the "point" of his essay is the closing anecdote. A perceptive and analytical reader senses immediately that the little story of the sergeant and the corporal is not the point of the essay at all. Woollcott has merely moved his analogic anecdote to the end of the essay instead of keeping it at the beginning; in so doing, he has forced the reader to look backward instead of forward from the anecdote. Therefore the anecdote itself occupies only the space proportionate to Woollcott's announced purpose in the prefatory gloss. There, he introduces the essay as "A parable setting forth one traveler's reflections on the vestigial remains of inequality which, to the loud delight of all conservatives, one does encounter in the Soviet Union."

Most of the time, Woollcott has no need for such contrivances. In essay after essay, the analogies alone are sufficiently fresh, appropriate, and felicitous to charm the reader. Normally, too, the introductory anecdotes work smoothly to help create the basic analogies, as in "The Little Fox-Terrier,"[19] which represents the Woollcottian essay at very nearly its best and which even includes the interesting effects of an appended letter from a chiropodist who had read the essay. In this very short piece, the sprightly and engaging anecdote of the opening paragraph makes possible an equally sprightly and engaging analogy that begins in the second paragraph, where Woollcott makes the cleverest possible use of the tale of the dejected fox terrier who, by standing on his head before an audience of children at a circus, stole the show from twenty-five elephants who were standing unnoticed on their heads. In writing of the attractions of the Chicago World's Fair, which is the true subject of this essay, Woollcott confesses that, though "the treasure chests of the world were ransacked for my pleasure," his real enjoyment was the World's Fair counterpart of the little fox terrier at the circus—the rickshaws and the rickshaw boys that carried one along the avenues of the great exposition.

As one might see from this sampling, one never knows what to expect from Woollcott, save that he usually manages a surprise and that he never runs out of the unexpected, however familiar or commonplace or trivial the subject might be. Perhaps this constant element of surprise is the main reason his readers never tired of reading his work. He began consciously working toward this goal during his first years as a *Times* cub when he found that he had little interest in purely reportorial writing. His flair for seeing and emphasizing the "human interest" values in his stories carried over into his work as a drama critic, where his familiarity with historical minutiae and other theatrical lore provided him with engaging anecdotes for all occasions and where his acquaintance with theatrical folk gave his criticism a personal touch, a gossipy tone, unavailable to those critics who held themselves aloof from the theater folk whom they criticized. By the time Woollcott left his job as drama critic for the *World* in 1928, he seemed as much a part of the theater as were the playwrights, producers, directors, and performers about whom he wrote.

III   Theater of War

Had he maintained an unbroken tenure as drama critic without ever having served on the *Stars and Stripes* during the First World War, however, it is less likely that his talents would have matured as they did or that his later career would have been so spectacular. Coming early in Woollcott's career as essayist and raconteur, yet at a time when his talents were most responsive to maturing influences, the war took him outside the close-boundaried arena of theatrical reviewing and brought him close to human beings under circumstances that stripped away the veneer of civilization, the luxury of art, and the pretensions of society. In the war camps and on the front lines, Americans were united under a high and universal purpose that deeply affected Woollcott and that allowed him to see ordinary people as he had never intimately known them before. For the first time he realized that, as a writer, he had been laboring under a supreme handicap: nothing in his experience of the world had made it possible for him to enter the minds and hearts of ordinary human beings, especially those of his own countrymen. "I think I first came to know mine own people," he wrote to Mrs. Truax, "in the woods near Chateau-Thierry."[20]

For these reasons, among several others, Woollcott's service with the American Expeditionary Force was a broadening, deepening, and highly satisfying experience. It was one of the happiest times of his life, not only because he felt keenly the "identification with a cause beyond dispute in value,"[21] nor only because he "achieved a feeling and respect for the tastes of the average American to whom he would direct his writings in the future,"[22] but because he learned that his readers would respond to his heightened and intensified sentiments only if they were genuine. If his stories for *Stars and Stripes* are told "in the manner of Ernie Pyle with an overlarding of Elsie Dinsmore,"[23] they are nonetheless charged with unmistakable conviction. "It was all in the superlative mood, all under high pressure," explains Samuel Hopkins Adams, "but it was saved by its utter sincerity. Woollcott more than believed every word he wrote: he felt it."[24]

In Woollcott's prefatory remarks to the collected *Stars and Stripes* despatches, which he published in 1919 under the title *The Command Is Forward*, his sincerity is unmistakable. Not ghoulishly, but with gratitude for the luck of the professional newspaperman, he speaks of the fortuitous circumstances by which he attained "a reserved seat at the war." At the same time, he also realizes that the handy metaphor of war as drama is, after all, only a figure of speech, that war is not an art form, but the grimmest of realities that is to be properly written about only by one who is part of it; and he is proud that those who write for the *Stars and Stripes* are "themselves enlisted men—privates for the most part." For Woollcott, then, the "theater of war" was real life seen in its most dramatic terms. *The Command Is Forward* contains experiments in most of the kinds of writing for which he became famous in his later years.

IV   The Command Is Forward

What he felt when he wrote the *Stars and Stripes* stories, and what he intended that his readers should feel every bit as keenly, were national pride and the highest degree of patriotic fervor: "I do believe with all my heart," he wrote Mrs. Truax, "there never were braver, gentler, finer, more chivalrous soldiers [than the Americans] since the world began."[25] But transcending this almost mandatory and rather obvious glorification of the American soldier were other emotions that Woollcott felt just as deeply—ones that were even more fundamental to the human condition at large. "In that strange simple country which was called the front," he observed with a touch of awe in "A Letter to the Folks" at the end of *The Command Is Forward,* there were no artificial lines separating human beings from each other, no superficial values, no sectional or geographical distinctions.

Acts of kindness and of valor in that "strange simple country," then, were a monument to the earthbound potential of the human spirit. To the Aleck Woollcott who had been an intellectual loner in high school and college, and to the Alexander Woollcott whose professional art had been forged in the glittering and sophisticated world of the Great White Way, the war was an experience both expanding and leveling to his talent. It provided the first revelation of his innate sympathy with the mind and heart of the common man, and it was the source of stories that required that he apply to a chronicling of that mind and heart all the artful devices that he had heretofore devoted to lives of celebrities and to criticism of the theater.

Of the thirty-five newspaper stories that constitute *The Command Is Forward,* ten can be categorized as panoramic reports of the major military engagements marking the advance of the American Expeditionary Force from Chateau-Thierry and Belleau Wood through the battles of the Aisne, St. Mihiel, Montsec, and the Meuse-Argonne—all between May and November of 1918. Though these reports are the most purely reportorial of all the items in the collection, these stories provide a basic pattern for what would otherwise be a random and heterogeneous assortment of impressions, ones without focus or progression. In pulling all his despatches together into a single collection, Woollcott demonstrated that, even as he wrote the stories chronologically day by day, his eye had never lost track of the vast movements of men and material under which were subsumed all the smallest individual thoughts, feelings, and actions of the war.

In writing these panoramic chapters, Woollcott tended to adopt the tone and spirit of the individual battles of the Classical epics; and while his accounts were appropriate to current taste, he adapted to these stories many of the tested devices of the epics: an elevated tone, a sense of massive simultaneous movements, individual heroics, quick glimpses of revealing and humanizing minutiae, and at times even the sense of cosmic or supernatural forces at work. The heroes of these small epic engagements, however, were no classic supermen or demigods; they were the American infantryman, the doughboy, who, as Woollcott declares in his preface, "bore the greatest burden, suffered the greatest hardship and privation, earned the greatest glory."

In his earliest panoramas, Woollcott experimented with ways by which he might employ varieties of restricted viewpoint to localize his material, even while that same viewpoint suggested the full scope of the action. In "One Man and a Battle Sixty Miles Long," he states that no man can describe the entire action along a sixty mile front, though "one who has been in the thick of it can tell at least what he did and saw and heard." Among those personal accounts that tell more "than all the maps and reports by military experts" is one told by a sergeant who protested that "after all, he had not had much to do with the fight." The sergeant's first person account, however, presents in close detail the typical moment-by-moment occurrences during a sleepless seventy-two hour advance along a front that stretched all the way from Soissons to Chateau-Thierry. Too, in "The St. Mihiel Picnic," Woollcott describes what an observer might have seen from a hilltop behind St. Mihiel on September 12, 1918: the rapid advance of eight American divisions under General Pershing. It was a "big, bouncing young army, armed to the teeth and the teeth themselves glistening in a supremely confident grin." This magnificently coordinated advance was so fast and smooth, remarks Woollcott, that "it was a little like a movie war."

Hereafter, for the most part, Woollcott accepted the role of a comprehensively informed observer, for he laced the broad panoramic passages with illuminating detail and anecdote. From this viewpoint, he provides chronologically sequential accounts of the action under the titles "Montsec," "The Meuse-Argonne Begins," "The Argonne Hills," "The Final Smash," and "Nach Sedan." Of the climactic phase of the occupation, the passing of the Rhine in "The Rhine at Last," Woollcott describes the American ceremonial march over the Bridge of Boats by an army which, by European standards of public ceremony, "simply refuses to be dramatic." According to Woollcott's account, the First Brigade crossed the river—Germany's historic "link of lore and legend"—led by a major on horseback who was followed in turn by a brigadier general, some French officers, a Young Womens' Christian Association girl with cookies and cigars, and a Chicago *Daily News* correspondent with his dog. The dog, "wearing an intent look . . . [was] bent, as it afterwards developed, on searching for the first lamp-post on the left bank."

The single characteristic of these panoramic war studies is that, collectively, though they capture the sweep and movement of the whole front, the memorable things are preserved in the details—in the dog's search, in heroic actions by individual soldiers, in lines of dialogue, in postures and attitudes, in unconsciously revealing words and gestures. True to form, Aleck was incapable of seeing the war in terms of maps and charts, strategy and statistics. To him, these were not the war at all. The people were the war. Only the people, both military and civilian, mattered.

For this reason, the basic structure of *The Command Is Forward* emerges as a chronological sequence of these panoramic stories, to each of which adheres a cluster of more highly specialized stories devoted to dramatizing the peculiar ways in which each of the major military engagements affected both the troops and the native inhabitants. Eight of the stories, for instance, concentrate upon the unique conditions under which the doughboys made various advances, or upon the cultural and psychological effects of the campaign both during the war and immediately after the armistice. These are "Forage," "The Battle of Dreadful Roads," "The Little Long-Lost Towns," "On the Frontier," "Encore Reveille," "The Life of Riley," "The Almighty Cake of Soap," and "The Wounds Begin to Heal."

In the ceaseless life-and-death brinkmanship of the battlefields, where, as Woollcott observes in his Preface, the scattered American troops first realized that they were part of "one great, onmoving, irresistible army," certain groups or units performed their duties with extraordinary heroism. In seven chapters of the collection, Woollcott accords these soldiers the full measure of glory. Five typical accounts are "Soldiers of the Telephone," "The Tanks," "The Winged Cameras," "The Runners," and "The Pioneers." In "The Argonne Players," as one might expect of a medical sergeant correspondent who was also a top flight drama critic, Woollcott pays tribute to the theatrical unit of the Seventy-Seventh Division from New York, whose permanent ingenue was a musical comedy "hoofer" named Harry Cahill. "Compared with the job of a troupe that must give two shows a day, rehearse in the mornings on a new one, do all its housework and carry all its own props," observes Woollcott, "the life of a stevedore is a life of flowery ease."

Of all the stories in this group, the account of "The Lost Battalion" is the most graphic and the most thoroughly charged with implication and emotion. The glory of the lost battalion has become one of the persistent legends of World War I, but at the time Woollcott wrote his article for *Stars and Stripes*, the incident was history of less than two weeks' vintage. Even in so short a time the episode had spawned some false twists of legend, like the report that Major Whittlesey had replied to the German surrender ultimatum by tossing back into the German lines a stone wrapped in paper containing the message "Go to Hell." Woollcott strips the account of such unproved interpolation, sensing that no embellishment could improve the dramatic facts of the episode. So he tells a sound and straightforward story of the battalion which, following orders, held a ravine for five full days without support or supply, were cut off from units that had failed to reach their assigned objectives, lived on leaves and were therefore too weak even to bury their dead, but nonetheless ignored a German order to surrender and were rescued only in the last moments before they expired from hunger and exhaustion. Among those stories that made the lost battalion an enduring chapter in American war lore, Woollcott's account must be considered one of the foremost.

Four of the stories in *The Command Is Forward* are concerned with heroic deeds of individuals, and most of these accounts are strongly sentimental, a vein that Woollcott was to mark as his own. The title of the book itself is taken from the opening chapter, hardly more than an anecdote, in which, with his last breath, a mortally wounded captain snaps to attention, delegates his authority to a lesser officer, and cries out to his men at the very moment of death, "The command is 'Forward.' "

The chapters about individual heroes are all, in one way or another, demonstrations of the undefeatable spirit of those who have heard, at least implicitly, such a command. That is the spirit of the fifteen year old soldier in "Scotty," just as it is that of the high-ranking heroes like Brigadier General Douglas MacArthur and Colonel William F. ("Wild Bill") Donovan in "The Irregular Army." Perhaps none of the soldier-heroes so touched the hearts of the foot soldiers, however, as did the actions of the two men of the cloth; one the now-famous Father O'Flaherty, the other, the French curé of St. Mihiel. The tribute to Father O'Flaherty appears in the form of a testimonial upon his death at Very in October of 1918. Woollcott records the remarks of the soldiers themselves, the climactic remark being, "He was too damned brave." And of the French priest Woollcott observes that the whole story of the four year bondage of the citizens in their own native town "can be told in terms of one man, the Curé-Doyen of St. Mihiel."

Of all the stories which comprise the thirty-five chapters of *The Command Is Forward,* those that caught the fancy of the general reading public were the three or four representatives of a Woollcottian literary formula that did much to establish his success in later years—the sentimental and the nostalgic sketch. "Madame Cocaud of Savenay," for example, is Woollcott's appreciative testimonial to the little French woman who, having lost her own son in the war, "seems to think of herself as a sort of special mess sergeant for the American Army." She pampered the doughboys with her delicacies, but she refused wine to a captain because her son had been a "simple soldat." "Eddie Grant's Last Game" is an account of the heroic death of a popular professional baseball player. As a member of a relief unit that worked among soldiers whose "minds had ceased to work, but their hearts had not," Captain Eddie Grant was killed while leading his men into relief action. In doing so, he gave his usual impression that "there never was any difference between the Eddie Grant who walked forward, smiling and unconcerned under shell-fire, and the Eddie Grant of old, trotting out from the bench to third base."

By far the most successful story in *The Command Is Forward,* in fact the most widely acclaimed in all seventy-one issues of *Stars and Stripes,*[26] was "Verdun Belle," a touching tale "of a trench dog who adopted a young leatherneck, of how she followed him to the edge of the battle around Chateau-Thierry, and was waiting for him when they carried him out." In the collected version, Woollcott describes her ancestry as simply "dubious," but in the widely read later version[27] she is a "shabby, lonesome dog—a squat setter bitch of indiscreet, complex, and unguessable ancestry." In the original version, Verdun Belle begins ministering to her lost warrior as soon as he is placed within her reach, so that "the first consciousness he had of his new surroundings was the feel of her rough pink tongue licking his face." In the elaborated later version, however, Woollcott adds a most effective sentimental touch. To the dog he attributes just the right thoughts and feelings of proprietary maternal exasperation: "here was this mess of a doughboy of hers to be washed up first. So like him to get all dirty the moment her back was turned."

This story has been anthologized and otherwise reprinted many times. For Woollcott, its tone and method became a model for the sentimental tales he wrote with adroitness and effect throughout his career as a free-lance writer and as a radio raconteur. "Ever since the late spring of 1918," wrote John T. Winterich in 1931, "Verdun Belle has been supporting Alexander Woollcott. Her story has become a byword and a barking. I have heard it in the watch-fires of a hundred circling camps; others have heard it around as many poker, bridge, cribbage and dinner tables; it has appeared in print (under various titles, but always over the signature of Alexander Woollcott) in virtually every American periodical except the *Wall Street Journal* and the Harvard *Alumni Monthly*."[28]

With such narratives as "Verdun Belle," Woollcott became something more than a converted drama critic and something more than a superior journalist. He was emerging as a superb storyteller whose best tales were to be founded upon actual occurrences or upon the reworking of legendary materials. For these purposes, his best training ground was the war, and it may even be said that, as a literary artist, he discovered the real scope and potential of his talent in writing his regular despatches from the front. Typically, he regarded these despatches more as "features" than as "reports," and their success among the doughboys, if not as a single collection among the home folk after the war, suggests both the accuracy of his judgment and the calibre of his writing.

As a collection, *The Command Is Forward* reveals something important that the individual *Stars and Stripes* despatches could not reveal about the special ways in which Woollcott's powers were developing. Though the overall purpose of the despatches was to keep the doughboys informed of all that was happening around them—to assure them that their efforts were part of some cogent plan, to increase their sense of oneness with each other and with their allies—and though Woollcott's stories served this larger strategic purpose well, the unforgettable things in *The Command Is Forward* are the apt details, the illuminating anecdotes, the unexpectedly relevant trivia whose sudden brilliance touches the deepest sensitivities.

As eyewitness records of the war, Woollcott's graphic accounts of the sweeping American advances are examples of excellent reporting and are valuable contributions to American history. But if these accounts are memorable at all, they are memorable for the small things that are linked only incidentally to the war and that show human beings speaking and behaving in ways recognizably common to the species: the boy in "Forage" who, "caught by a splinter from a random shell, died with a smile on his face and a wing of fried chicken in his fist"; the troops in "Montsec" who stormed the fortress created by a "disembowelled hill" and found "no living creature on Montsec, save one affable internationalist setter, now variously known as Fritz and Montsec, and four blinking rabbits, penned against a shortage of rations"; Sergeant Gowdy in "The Life of Riley," who "took two baths last week, which doubled his bathing average for the year"; the children in "The Wounds Begin to Heal" who were found "masquerading for Mardi Gras in discarded American gas masks" and playing "with forgotten hand grenades"; the young draftee in "The Eleventh of November" who had undergone six months of grueling training and reached the front on the day the war ended; the old French woman in "The Little Long-Lost Towns" who stood "among the ruins of her home" and declared to passing doughboys, "Mon Dieu, a house can be rebuilt. It is not so with the life of a man"; and at least one good example of what later became the proved Woollcottian technique of discovering celestial reverberations in the most patently terrestrial of occurrences, as with Captain Leahy's behavior upon being hit through the breast with a large shell in the titular sketch, "The Command Is Forward." As might be expected, his head sagged before he died; but as he verbally relinquished his command, he straightened up for a second and held up his head. "It was as if, somewhere in the universe, a Commander Invisible had called 'Attention!'"

V   *The Woollcott Trick*

By the time Woollcott returned to his old post as *Times* drama critic in New York in 1919, the various literary devices that together constitute the "Woollcott trick" had coalesced into a distinctive style and method of story telling. For these purposes, Woollcott thought almost exclusively in anecdotes; and, as John Mason Brown has observed, "He seldom told one story at a time. His anecdotes came not singly but in dynasties. He approached his main story through a labyrinth of lesser ones."[29] Too, as his wartime writings amply demonstrate, he frequently aspired to his peak performances through undisguised sentiment and nostalgia, and these achievements were strongly supported by coincidence or by the sense that the smallest episodes in the lives of men are somehow directed by the stars. This latter tendency probably explains the timeless, fairy tale aura of his most popular pieces. It may explain also his perception that life's most trivial things are frequently more significant than those that seem epoch making—if the trivia can be seen in true perspective.

Of Woollcott's fondness for bizarre crimes and for variations upon the Great American Success Story, there are dozens of instances among his tales; and as a salesman of his own enthusiasms, he has few peers in our literature. At whatever literary task he turned his hand, of course, his success must be counted largely the result of his sheer skill in the use of language. "At his best he used the language as one who loved it; at worst as one who was infatuated with it" wrote John Mason Brown,[30] and, whether in achieving the most appealing sentiment or the most devastating wit, Woollcott's keen sense of the subleties of language served him well.

For this reason, he remains America's prince of the retold tale. Seven years after his death, the private secretary of his free-lance years publicly confessed that "most of his anecdotes were already stale when they achieved the dignity of Joe Miller's Joke Book, but there is this maddening thing about the man: he is a master of English writing and can weave these ancient wheezes into such a spell of words that one not only does not resent this chicanery but, in his own language, clasps the threadbare anecdotes to one's bosom and treasures them for what they are—literature."[31]

Not only can Woollcott perform this magic, but the "ancient wheezes" are often his own renditions; they are told and retold and told again without significant change from version to version. The true monument to his skill as raconteur is that he could thus endlessly confront his wide-flung public without apology and leave skeptical and even jaded American readers happy as children with their bedtime stories.

CHAPTER 3

The Free Critic

IN the winter of 1914 when Woollcott wrote his first dramatic criticism for the *Times*, he was only twenty-seven years old—and he was by considerable odds the youngest first string drama critic on Broadway. His succession to the drama critic's desk was a fortuitous but a momentous event in his career, for out of "youthful diffidence"[1] he had not applied for the position. Yet eventually, as a recent biographer has observed, "it was as a critic that he exercised his greatest force in America."[2]

In the two and a half years before he entered the war, Woollcott devoted himself to becoming personally involved in the theatrical world about which he was expected to write and to sharpening the tools he intended to employ in writing about it. He had no doubts concerning what he wanted to do and little hesitation in doing it; but he knew he must overcome serious obstacles if he were to adopt the style and the tone of language that he wanted to use. When theater historians say that Woollcott introduced a "new voice" into dramatic criticism, they use the phrase more literally than one might suspect; for his special service to dramatic criticism was that he made significant alterations in its focus, purpose, and range of appeal, all of which depended partly upon a distinct change in the "tone" that had characterized dramatic criticism in America.

I Clash with Tradition

Heretofore, criticism of the theater had been basically elitist; but Woollcott had no patience with the ponderous and elevated "classical" tone and vocabulary perpetuated into the first decades of the twentieth century by the venerable William Winter (and his sometimes unwitting proteges) whose criticism reflected the conditions of a time when the theater had tended to be the province of the rich, the well-educated, and the leisure classes. Perceiving that the the-

67

ater had become part of the fabric of American life rather than a form of embroidery upon it, Woollcott desired to write the kind of criticism that would both inform and entertain a much broader segment of the regular news-reading public than his predecessors and most of his contemporaries had ever envisioned. To Woollcott had fallen the task of popularizing dramatic criticism without allowing its quality—both as value judgment and as a special literary form—to fall below that of the brilliant but literati-oriented reviews and essays by such contemporary practitioners as Percy Hammond and George Jean Nathan.

From his first appearances as a recognized drama critic, Woollcott stirred the theatrical world with the sense that something different and disturbing occupied the first nighters' seats. Although he was surprisingly knowledgeable in the ways of the contemporary theater and could readily detect bad acting, directing, and producing, he was unashamedly enthralled with the theatrical world, as he had been from his childhood years as a playgoer with Roswell Field in Kansas. His impulse was always to praise the theater first and to condemn afterward, or even, if his integrity permitted, to praise without any condemnation. Since his eye rarely missed grievous faults in any theatrical production, he soon became feared for his capacity to detect the flaws that players and directors recognized in their work, but which they strove to conceal from their audiences.

Moreover, Woollcott was wholly out of sympathy with one of the most solidly entrenched of the self-imposed traditions among the critics—a tradition that was at that time a sore issue in the profession because theater management had charged some of the older critics with flagrantly violating it. This tradition had grown out of the generally accepted belief that no drama critic could retain his integrity or his credibility if he made friends or had any business dealings whatever with theater managers, if he attended rehearsals of the plays he must judge as a public critic, if he had any knowledge at all of playwrights and their scripts before the productions were mounted, and above all if he consorted with actors and actresses in his private life. Most of the first line critics so regarded this tradition as an occupational fiat that they prided themselves upon an objectivity that arose from their lack of personal involvement in the art they criticized. As far as possible, they even policed their own ranks. Indeed, when the *Times* sent Woollcott to London and to the Continent as part of his formal preparation as a critic, Burns Mantle met him in Paris and passed on the standard advice. Woollcott, of course, would have none of it.

Unforeseeably, then, in ways that went far beyond the appointment of a new drama critic, Van Anda's selection of Woollcott was as important a decision for the *Times* as for the critic. Though the executive staff of the paper had acquired ample confidence in Woollcott as a newsman and writer, nobody on the staff could yet have recognized what a formidable adversary, and therefore what a valuable ally, he could be in a fight. The owner, the editor, and the young drama critic of the *Times* formed a professional alliance powerful enough to shatter long-held precedents, to help establish important legal rulings, and to alter the function of dramatic reviewing in America.

In the light of events that developed from Woollcott's appointment as a critic, it is difficult to understand how thoroughly underrated the office of dramatic criticism was in 1914. Woollcott's immediate predecessor, Adolph Klauber, had been a competent critic, but neither a flashy nor an inspired one, during a period when the *Times* was not among the most affluent or influential newspapers in New York. To its executive and editorial staffs, the drama critic had served the wholly routine function of reviewing plays for which theater managers offered free tickets, in partial exchange for the most expensive advertising space in the paper. If a critic dared indulge his integrity by writing a damaging review, the managers followed a fairly well-established practice of barring that critic from their theaters or even of withdrawing their advertising until the newspaper had muzzled the wayward critic. The best critics of the time managed to show both the good and the bad in the plays they saw, but they rode a thin line between the expression of truth and the avoidance of offense.

The opportunity to which Woollcott had aspired all his life—the one that fell his way by accident when Klauber married Jane Cowl and decided to become a producer—offered a seat of only questionable advantage during the first decade or so of the twentieth century. Most newspaper publishers felt uneasy in the hiring of honest, knowledgeable, and strong-minded drama critics; the value of criticism was clouded by the scorn and distrust of theater managers; and the responsibilities of the critics were hedged about by long-standing circumscriptions and taboos. Relationships between the theater and the public were changing rapidly in the second decade of the century, however, and to Woollcott and the *Times* fell the mandate to challenge the established order.

In succeeding Klauber, Woollcott joined a critical fraternity that had been recently under fire for alleged dishonesty and even incompetence. These charges had been leveled by Marc Klaw of the Klaw and Erlanger group of theaters, and the charges were immediately amplified and perpetuated by the theatrical community through articles in *The Billboard*. Without mentioning names, Klaw had accused four New York critics of conferring together after performances in order to agree upon what they would write in their drama columns. Then, speaking for theatrical managers, *The Billboard* attacked drama critics in general by calling them egotistical and incompetent and by declaring that the job of drama critic was too lowly a journalistic post to attract honorable and competent writers.[3]

Yet within weeks after Woollcott began writing his *Times* drama columns, readers, playgoers, and other critics were aware that dramatic reviewing had acquired a writer of taste and excellence. He made no radical changes in the basic format of the drama pages, for he had inherited only the daily reviewing columns and the special Sunday column that Klauber had filled during Woollcott's years as a "cub." Moreover, though Klauber's tenure as drama critic had at last earned for him a by-line on the Sunday column, the *Times* was habitually reluctant to award by-lines; and, as a result of this policy, Woollcott began his career as drama critic without a signature on either the daily reviews or the larger and more comprehensive Sunday columns.

He managed, however, to do several things that would later identify his work unmistakably. Under Klauber, for instance, neither the daily nor the weekly column had its own special heading. The editors apparently worked out different headings for each issue, just as they did for every occasional article in the issue. But under Woollcott's management, both columns soon moved nearer the front of the paper and appeared with standard boxed headings—the daily reviews titled "The Play," and the Sunday essays titled "Second Thoughts on First Nights." Previously, too, during Klauber's regime, the *Times* maintained only one drama critic to cover opening nights at the thirty or so theaters in New York. If two openings occurred on the same night, Klauber was forced to commandeer the services of a writer from some other department of the paper (there is no record that he ever called upon Woollcott for this chore). This haphazard and unreliable method Woollcott soon corrected by convincing Van Anda that the paper would profit by hiring away Brock Pemberton, the second string critic for the *World,* a keen young journalist for whom Woollcott had acquired some liking and respect during their simultaneous tours of English and Continental theaters. Pemberton was the first in a succession of Woollcott's underlings on various newspapers, many of whom—like John Corbin, George S. Kaufman, Alison Smith, and Jeffrey Holmesdale (Lord Amherst)—were to follow notable careers of their own in theater-connected enterprises.

But at best these advancements in location, format, and personnel were of secondary importance compared with the impact of Woollcott's literary style and his techniques of review and criticism. Though he was the newest and youngest drama critic in New York, no other contemporary critic could match the avid and sustained interest in the theater that Woollcott had brought with him from his earliest years. Moreover, few had greater knowledge of modern theatrical history; few, if any, had equal quickness of perception; and none could so well adapt the English language to the special purposes of dramatic criticism. And, within a few years after Woollcott's appointment as critic, none of his brotherhood on Broadway could compete with his intimate acquaintance with theatrical personalities or with his esoteric knowledge of current theatrical affairs in Europe or in America.

II *Technique of the Mixed Review*

In the winter of 1914, when the freshman critic on Broadway settled into a taxing regimen of first night playgoing and reviewing, he began systematically working out the best ways of reaching the goals he had set for himself. Like all drama critics during that era of proliferating stage production, Woollcott found that the glamour of constant playgoing was more than offset by the boredom that arose from the sameness of the routine. For most play reviewers, he discovered, life was a constant struggle against the tendency to become irretrievably jaded.

The theater of the time, he quickly perceived, was motivated far more by commercialism than by a desire for artistic excellence. Truly fine performances were scarce indeed. So bad was the common run of plays, in fact, that only a critic of the most resilient intellect and the most irrepressible respect for the theater could keep his critical sense from warping. The necessary and practical antidote to that danger was, of course, a determined optimism; and according to Woollcott, the battery of Broadway critics was "the incorrigibly hopeful part of every first audience, pathetically eager to believe that something fine and memorable is about to be discovered in the next act."[4] Moreover, as Woollcott soon recognized, if critics were able to keep their perspective under the constant bombardment of bad and mediocre productions, that very stability became the foundation for their most incontrovertible authority as professional drama critics: "If your professional playgoer seems to think that a fair farce is good and a good melodrama superb, it is probably because only he knows how bad a play can be. He grows delirious about the best in the theater because he alone knows the worst."[5]

Even so, Woollcott kept his perspective so well that his reviews and criticisms were seldom the pure "raves" of what he had called "betrousered Pollyannas" nor the almost unleavened "damnations" characterized by the "venom from contented rattlesnakes" which had been said to drip from the pen of Percy Hammond (See Adams, p. 98). To Woollcott, the prime function of the competent drama critic was to be perceptive and analytical—to serve as one of "the public's faithful scouts,"[6] whose task was "to separate and weigh the various factors"[7] that were responsible for the success or failure of any stage production as a work of art.

Accordingly, though from time to time Woollcott waxed either ecstatic or vituperous about some performer or some director or some aspect of the "investiture" of a production, he became the grand master of the "mixed review." To his critical sense, any generalized and indiscriminate approval or condemnation of a dramatic production was an abrogation of the critic's responsibility. Since the process of mounting a play involved dozens of separate artistic problems, some factors tended to be strong and some to be weak when the whole production became an entity of its own. It was a most unusual performance, then, in which all these complex matters were equally good or equally bad.

During his first two or three years as a critic, he perceptibly exerted his resources to find sound but entertaining methods of expressing these mixed views—to devise ways of making similar assessments over and over for different plays without appearing repetitive. To his ingenuity in solving the latter problem goes much credit for the constantly fresh flavor of his prose and for the sustained interest of his readers. In these respects he was so successful that, during more than a dozen years of constant playgoing, some of his contemporaries insisted that his columns were always more entertaining than the plays themselves.

One of the unmistakable characteristics of Woollcott's reviews is what Hoyt calls the "time bomb" effect[8] that arises from two forces working together: from the necessity for Woollcott to find some principle of order among the strong and the weak elements in each play he reviewed, and from his lifelong tendency to experiment with order and proportion to achieve the strongest effect in whatever he wrote. The "time bomb" was most devastating when Woollcott began by praising the good things in a performance and then switched into an intensive exploration of the weaknesses, which in the long run might amount to an overwhelming condemnation of the play as whole. He achieved the opposite effect by opening with a disheartening examination of a play's shortcomings, only to shift unexpectedly into exultant praise of other things. In extreme cases, he was entirely capable of spending most of his space in a discussion of either praiseworthy or blameable matters, only to finish by making the opposite recommendation on the basis of a single, pervasive factor that in his judgment more than overshadowed all the rest. To his credit, however, these shifts of ground rarely seemed fey or arbitrary. For the most part, he wrote with conviction; and he justified his views by means of keen observation, good taste, and sound judgment.

Ordinarily, he reserved the "time bomb" technique for reviews of plays that were poorly balanced or badly proportioned or uneven. Plays of this kind sometimes have a great deal of unrealized potential, or they are extraordinarily good in some ways and insufferably bad in others. For instance, in his review of F. H. Rose's *The Whispering Well* ("The Play," October 6, 1920), Woollcott opens with an encouraging discussion of the history of the play and of how it had reached Broadway; and he casually describes the piece as "a handsomely decorated and sufficiently well-played folk fantasy." But now, beyond the halfway point and just before an objective summary of the plot, he says baldly that the drama is "a trite and singularly insipid morality play, which limped painfully because of clumsy stage management, but which would have had a hard time seeming beautiful and significant under any circumstances."

Similarly, in his review of Zona Gale's drama *Miss Lulu Bett* ("The Play," December 28, 1920), he begins by praising the novel from which the novelist herself had made the play. Then he describes the mood of happy anticipation with which the novel readers in the audience welcomed the adaptation, and he praises Brock Pemberton for his shrewdness in casting. Just beyond this point, and more than halfway through the review, the unwary reader assumes that the review is meant to be a highly complimentary one. But now Woollcott fires the hidden charge that he has been saving when he announces that the "stray visitor," who has never read the novel, would find "a rather dull and flabby play, one somewhat sleazily put together by a playwright who has but aught sense of dramatic values and no instinct at all for the idiom of the theatre."

He became singularly adroit at saving the "time bomb" for exactly the right moment, and he seemed never to tire of devising unexpected ways to insinuate the sudden shift of tone at the right place. All in all, a reader never knew what to expect from a Woollcott review until he had finished reading it; and for theater people, the reading of a Woollcott review could be nerve wracking. The impulse of an actor who read a Woollcott review of his own performance was to hold his breath until he discovered when, if ever, the "time bomb" was exploded.

Woollcott did not, however, use this device only for its dramatic effect. In many ways, his method was the natural and perhaps the inevitable product of a reviewing technique designed to provide fair and balanced estimates of professional dramatic performances. If, in the process of dissection, Woollcott tended to find something laudable in the worst of plays and something faulty in the best, and if he composed his reviews to make the most of the comparative values, the result was usually as fair an assessment as any critic could give. Too, if his general reactions were overbalanced in any direction, they leaned in favor of the actors and actresses, for whom he had much compassion and toward whose performances he was sometimes more lenient than the players deserved.

III   *Reviewing Under Injunction*

But in the minds of theater managers, Woollcott's insistence upon balanced reviewing was anathema. The management could not hope to sell its wares so long as critics like Woollcott persevered in telling the public honestly about all the bad things in the plays along Broadway. Moreover, it was obvious that Woollcott could not be corrupted into writing reviews that might be used as advertising for bad or mediocre plays, for most managers relied on such "advertising" to help them make as much money as possible out of a bad play before it closed. Perhaps it was inevitable, and in retrospect it does not appear surprising, that Woollcott would at some time find himself in open conflict with one or another of the big theater management companies in New York. Nor is it surprising that the conflict was precipitated, as has been noted, by the powerful Shubert brothers, Jake and Lee. The only surprise is that the attack occurred before Woollcott was a mature critic and before the *Times* itself was among the most powerful of the New York newspapers.

As Woollcott went about his necessary tasks in the early spring of 1915, nothing in the routine theatrical affairs on Broadway suggested that he would be selected for what the Shuberts apparently intended to be an object lesson. At that time, an ordinary run of plays occupied the New York theaters; and among them was *Taking Chances*, a new farce featuring an actor named Lou-Tellegen, whose principal qualification was that he had recently been Sarah Bernhardt's leading man. The play was announced as usual in the Sunday edition of the *Times* on March 14, along with other plays on the first night calendar. So far, everything seemed perfectly normal. The first indication that the Shuberts were testy about this particular production was a special theatrical advertisement—in a bordered box underneath the standard advertisement for *Taking Chances*—which appeared in the *Times* on March 18, the morning after the first performance, in the same issue as Woollcott's review. Since the notice also appeared in fourteen other metropolitan newspapers on that day, the Shuberts had obviously composed and submitted this special notice before they had seen reviews by any critics who had attended the first performance.

This highly irregular notice sought to assure prospective viewers that even though "some of the critics, lacking in humor," might say disparaging things about *Taking Chances*, the first performance of the play had "scored one of the most sensational comedy hits ever known in an American theatre." Beyond the obvious fact that the Shuberts had submitted the notice before the opening, and therefore could not have known at that time what the audience response actually would be, the reviews of the critics indicated that the show was among the least satisfactory of the season. In fact, the only review that was encouraging appeared in the Shubert house organ, the *New York Review*. In the regular press, there were six "hedging" or purely descriptive reviews and eight basically adverse and potentially damaging reviews, including Woollcott's in the *Times*.

Of these eight reviews, Woollcott's was not the most disparaging. Neither an exceptionally good nor an exceptionally bad piece of Woollcott writing, it was a reasonably typical example of the Woollcott brand of review. His most serious indictment concerned the play itself—the kind of inept translation from a foreign language (in this case, from the German) against which he waged continual war throughout his career as a critic. Labeling the play "a bedroom farce," he accused the translators of indulging chiefly in "a process of laborious deletion" from the original German drama and of thereby preparing a play that was "quite absurd and little more than that."

In particular, he was offended by the structurally important second act, for it consisted "of uninterrupted conversation and is one of those trying scenes that seem to owe their ability to proceed at all only to the providential circumstance that the woman in the case is no more than half-witted." On the other hand, Woollcott had many compliments to pay. Lou-Tellegen was "an ever interesting figure on the stage" and considerable portions of his performance were "deft and pleasing." In Ivy Troutman's performance as the lady, there were "some very skillful moments." The play was more than adequately mounted, and the director had demonstrated "a sure and able hand."

In his usual fashion, Woollcott was carefully selective; and he presented concrete and knowledgeable reasons for the things that offended his taste and good sense, even if he did not always feel it necessary to defend his sometimes fulsome enthusiasms. Altogether, his review of *Taking Chances* was as fair and balanced an assessment as an obviously weak play deserved. But reduced to its elements, the message of the review was unmistakable: despite good acting, directing, and general investiture, the play itself was execrable; for those components could not make the stage production satisfactory.

The Shuberts immediately retaliated by invoking the classic wrist-slapping device of barring Alexander Woollcott from attending plays produced in any of the Shubert theaters, but the *Times* was welcome to send any other critic to cover Shubert plays. Historically, and even according to the practice of the day, this action was by no means unusual, since most theater magnates had from time to time banished willful critics from their houses and since the Shuberts had already entered into this game with gusto. In New York, at one time or another, theaters had barred Channing Pollock,

Heywood Broun, Gilbert Gabriel, and Walter Winchell; in Chicago, Charles Collins; in Boston, both Philip Hale and George Holland; in Kansas City, Goodman Ace.

To retaliate, the most stubborn and ingenious among these excommunicated critics carried on long private vendettas in order to find ways of attending plays in the forbidden theaters. Pollock employed endless disguises to sneak past the doormen; but Walter Winchell had surpassed Pollock's best efforts by wearing Harpo Marx's blond wig and by entering through the stage door. In Boston, George Holland became an acting fire marshall who officially inspected the theaters only on opening nights.[9] One way or another, most of the banished critics managed to keep writing their reviews, at least sporadically; and although most of them were reinstated after a time, some were forced to compromise with Shubert demands in order to do so.

To the Shuberts, Woollcott may have seemed a particularly advantageous target in mid-March of 1915. Though as yet untried in the warfare of the theatrical marketplace, he was becoming so alarmingly popular with the theatergoing public that the *Times* theater page was becoming more and more important. The Shuberts had no reason to expect extraordinary trouble from *Times* publisher Adolph Ochs, but in a little over a decade he had staffed the paper with superior editors and journalists, and to the Shuberts, who were always sensitive to the ebb and flow of influences in the theatrical world, both the *Times* and its flashy young drama critic seemed to be moving rapidly toward positions of special power in the metropolis. However, the *Times* organization still appeared vulnerable to tactics that had already disturbed and partly defeated the most formidable newspapers in town.

Like several others who made the same mistake later, the Shuberts underestimated Woollcott's integrity, his perseverance, and his capacity to inspire in his own allies an extraordinary degree of confidence and loyalty. In this particular situation, if fighting alone, he could only have fought the Shuberts as all other banned critics had done before—by sneaking into the theaters under one subterfuge or another and by hoping to defeat his oppressors by his own ingenuity. If some such private campaign had failed, Woollcott's career as an honest and free-willed critic would have been over almost before it had begun. The Shuberts, well schooled in such matters, apparently expected Woollcott to play the game with all the odds in their favor. But, as they were to discover, Woollcott rarely did the expected thing when he was attacked. Throughout the long and widely publicized feud that followed, he made no attempt to enter any Shubert theater by force, subterfuge, disguise, or any other demeaning and vaudevillean device. Instead, he worked openly, with the support and the instructions of his paper, and pursued his business with purpose, reserve, appropriate dignity—and without personal rancor.

At first, until the paper could settle upon a course of action, Van Anda merely returned to the Shuberts and their managers all the complimentary tickets for reviewers, since the duly appointed representative of the *Times* was Alexander Woollcott. Meanwhile, following the suggestions of Van Anda, Woollcott went to Shubert box offices and purchased tickets for orchestra seats as any other customer might have done. But, no matter how often he presented these tickets, Jake Shubert's doormen turned him away. At the same time, Woollcott continued reviewing plays in all the non-Shubert houses, and his reputation as a perceptive and entertaining critic kept growing. In the long run, his service to the Shubert competitors was more than the Shuberts could tolerate financially.

To the Shuberts and to the theater community nationwide, however, the immediate shocker came when the *Times*—with what is now recognizable as traditional *Times* integrity and independence—did what no other newspaper had felt justified in doing under those circumstances. Publisher Ochs, editor Van Anda, and critic Woollcott fought back with weapons unthinkable to theater management. They not only obtained an injunction against the Shuberts, but they seized the prerogative always claimed by the theater managers: the publisher rejected all the Shubert advertising, and the business world of the American theater was shaken to its foundations. An injunction could be fought in the courts, but advertising was purely a matter of private negotiation. It was one thing for a manager or a producer to withhold his precious advertising in a fit of spite and then to reinstate it whenever he chose, but it was altogether unimagineable that a newspaper might reject it and reserve to itself the conditions of reinstatement. Worse yet, having gained the advantage of acting on the offensive, the *Times* made the whole situation a public issue by loading its columns with every piece of information relevant to either side of the case.

Fully supported by Ochs and Van Anda, Woollcott also registered against the Shuberts a legal action under the Civil Rights Statute;

and, protected by a court injunction on April 3, 1915, he attended a performance of *Trilby* at the Shubert Theater. The next day, beneath the headline "Reviewing a Play Under Injunction," the *Times* carried a survey of the circumstances of the case, along with the complaint registered by Woollcott and the full text of the court order. Accompanying this story was Woollcott's review of *Trilby*—and for the first time one of his daily reviews was conspicuously labeled "By Alexander Woollcott." Not only to the public at large but in the way best understood by theater people, the *Times* had committed itself to its critic and to freedom of the press.

Among the seven allegations in Woollcott's complaint was the declaration that "the defendants have thus discriminated against the plaintiff solely because they profess to be displeased with a dramatic criticism written by him . . . which criticism was in all respects temperate and reasonable and within the bounds of legitimate and proper criticism." Accordingly, Justice Bijur's order temporarily restrained the Shuberts from "denying to the plaintiff any of the accommodations, advantages, or privileges of any . . . place of public amusement enjoyed by the general public."

Woollcott's review of the 1915 revival of *Trilby* is interesting for a number of reasons besides the fact that it was made possible only by a court order. The story of Trilby had been one of Woollcott's favorites from his childhood days when his first public school teacher had been disturbed to find her precocious charge devouring George du Maurier's popular and sophisticated novel about the sinister Svengali. Throughout his life, Woollcott spoke of du Maurier as among his favorite novelists, along with Dickens and Miss Alcott. Therefore, when the injunction admitted him to a dramatic adaptation of *Trilby*, Woollcott was able to review it not only with affection but also with a degree of authority unusual even among New York's most erudite critics.

As it happened, he was generally pleased with the performance he saw at the Shubert Theater that night; but, lest his public think a favorable review might be the result of pressure from an injunction, he was careful to call upon his long familiarity with the story to provide a historical and dramatic basis for the things he liked most in the present production. Because this performance was a revival of a dramatic adaptation that had first appeared twenty years earlier and that had been revived once ten years before, Woollcott found a number of favorable comparisons, even though he could hardly have seen the earliest productions himself. Knowing that the previous productions had been generally successful. Woollcott noted with pleasure that several members of the earlier casts were continuing in the new production. Indeed, he felt that the play was well cast, and he said so. Wilton Lackaye was again playing the role of Svengali, and his "memorable third act has lost none of its old force"; and Leo Dietrichstein's performance had "grown in grace" since the first production. But the most gratifying performance to Woollcott was that of Phyllis Nielson-Terry, a newcomer to the role of Trilby, who for the first time in the history of *Trilby* productions was able to sing "Ben Bolt" without the dubbing of a voice from backstage.

Though the play could not stand comparison with du Maurier's book, and though it was therefore "ever heavily dependent on an entire familiarity with that story for the full sympathy and understanding of the people on the other side of the footlights," the first night audience was enthusiastic. All in all, according to Woollcott, the performance was "well worth going to—even if you have to get in by the aid of an injunction." This review is also a good early example of the ways in which Woollcott was already at work as both a dramatic and a literary critic. Here, as with increasing frequency in later years, Woollcott wrote as familiarly of a novel as of any dramatic adaptation made from one. When the time came, he found it no great leap from dramatic criticism to the informative and entertaining discussion of other literary forms.

IV   *The Shubert Showdown*

The nationally publicized court battle involving the *Times*, Woollcott, and the Shuberts continued for nearly a year before it was legally put to an uneasy rest by an appellate court reversal of the previous ruling, which had been in favor of Woollcott. The events of those months were crowded, hectic, suspenseful, and sometimes sadly comic. On April 8, the *Times* carried nearly a full page of material concerning the previous day's court arguments for and against the continuation of the injunction, and the material cited the Shubert counsel's reference to adverse reviews as evidence of Woollcott's "rancor and malice and venom." There were also "sidelight" articles, mostly in favor of Woollcott, that were dramatic enough in tone and content to let the nationwide theater public know that Woollcott's real life legal battle was as suspenseful as any "courtroom drama" in the American theaters.[10]

On April 10, Woollcott's counsel tendered affidavits defending Woollcott's reviews against the charges of malice and bias,[11] but on

April 15 the judge set aside the injunction that had admitted Woollcott to the Shubert theaters,[12] and it was more than a month before he found in favor of Woollcott. At that time, however, he stayed all other actions pending a Shubert appeal,[13] which was slated for argument on June 18,[14] at which time Woollcott's counsel argued that the Shuberts' motive was either plain spite or fear that truthful reviews might damage "what they regard as their sacrosanct private enterprise."[15] Nonetheless, on July 9 the Appellate Division reversed the original verdict by ruling that equal rights had no jurisdiction in that case,[16] or, as the *Harvard Law Review* later phrased it, "equity will not protect mere rights of personality as distinguished from property interests."[17]

The whole case was made the more spectacular by a series of related events that constantly increased the pressure on the Shuberts. Two of these events were the pending "Mills Bill," which was intended to protect critics from intimidation but which Jake Shubert's personal lobbying defeated by a snap vote without discussion of "the merits of the measure,"[18] and a federal investigation of the "syndicated" Shubert theaters under the Sherman antitrust law.[19] Other closely related actions were an injunction against the use of the title *Taking Chances* by a man who had previously produced "a clean, wholesome play" of that name;[20] dozens of reprinted letters from readers decrying the smothering of "honest criticism";[21] and the Shuberts' loss of lease for the Hippodrome, "the largest playhouse in New York,"[22] to Charles Dillingham.

Even though Woollcott had lost the case on a technicality, he eventually won in almost every other respect. To the public, Woollcott's colorful and tenacious stand for honest criticism had been accorded "almost as much space in the national press as another 'incident' taking place at the same time—World War I"[23]—and he had won the battle for public support by a wide margin. Moreover, the Woollcott affair had proved to the world that, even though theater management might prevail in the courtroom, its real master was not so much statutory law as the good will of a sensitive and fickle public that looked to the critics for both guidance and entertainment.

Barred from the Shubert theaters, Woollcott continued to view the plays presented by other managers. As his columns increased in popularity, all the other managers benefited, while the Shuberts perceptibly faded from public awareness. After a few months, even before Woollcott could appeal the finding of the courts, the

Shuberts served notice that Woollcott would again be acceptable as a critic in the Shubert theaters.

By means of his own burgeoning popularity as a public figure and as a writer, Woollcott had hit the Shubert empire where it could least stand injury—in the box office. But more important to Woollcott, he had emerged from the whole business with a heightened public image. He had set his own stage for a career as one of the best-known writers of his day. The American public could believe in Alexander Woollcott.

CHAPTER 4

One Fat Fate

A S a professional reviewer of plays in metropolitan New York City, Woollcott found the world of arts and letters open to him; and because he regarded the theater as a synthesis of the arts, his early years as a newspaper reviewer and critic were those in which he cultivated all the best things in his career. During fifteen years of his professional life, he was the first string drama critic for one or another of the leading metropolitan newspapers—a little more thàn eight years for the *Times*, three for the *Herald*, and three for the *World*—before he left a life in journalism that had grown too narrow for his interests as a writer.

During his prewar years on the *Times*, except for his book on Mrs. Fiske, he published his criticism almost exclusively in the newspaper. But shortly after he returned from the war to his old position on the *Times*, he began writing sketches and articles for the top flight magazines of that era. In this enterprise he was so rapidly successful that, by the time he left the *Times* in 1922, he was writing prolifically for the magazines; and while he remained officially the first string drama critic for the *Herald* and then for the *World*, most of his best criticism—both dramatic and literary—was being steadily collected from the newspapers and the magazines to help fill the widely read books that began to appear under his name. Three of his early books—*Shouts and Murmurs* (1922), *Enchanted Aisles* (1924), and *Going to Pieces* (1928)—are either largely or entirely gleaned from his previously published writings on the theater or on theater personalities. For his work during the years after he had left the *Times*, the best of his criticism of the theater is found in those collections.

I *The Dramatic Review as Belles-Lettres*

Though he remained an inseparable part of the theatrical scene even after he had abandoned the critic's desk for the writing table of the free lance, he had learned his trade, made his reputation, and become generally regarded as "the country's most respected drama critic"[1] by grinding out thousands of individual reviews and hundreds of weekly drama pages for the various metropolitan dailies for which his name alone was sometimes powerful enough to insure the interest of a wide and fervent readership. Among the members of his select and highly competitive profession, he became the generally acknowledged leader in raising the dramatic review from semi-commercial journalism to a minor form of belles-lettres that required of its writer good judgment, keen and honest analytic sense, depth and breadth of perspective, a regard for form, and, above all, the unerring diction and the curious felicity of phrasing that mark a superior style.[2]

Eventually he gained unprecedented popularity and considerable prestige as a writer of more substantial forms of dramatic and literary criticism, as a biographer of celebrities, as a collaborator with famous playwrights, and as the prolific author of highly personalized and widely read informal tales, sketches, and essays. But most of these later developments grew naturally from the peculiar range of topics forced upon him by his daily reviewing, by the avid interest with which he seized upon these subjects, by his penchant for pursuing the most exciting of them into such esoteric holes and corners of hidden information as would eventually make him an authority in writing of them, and by the consciousness of style by which he managed to keep sharp the public interest in a literary vehicle so mechanical and repetitive as the daily drama review.

In the beginning, Woollcott's world was the theatrical world—anything to do with any part of the theatrical world. He did more than ignore his profession's arcane but long-held edict against a critic's associating with people of the theater; he shredded that edict and flaunted the tatters before the eyes of his public. He was proud to be the accepted companion and confidant of producers, directors, playwrights, and stars. In his time, he was the prized and intimate friend of many of the brightest luminaries of the stage. And to the confounding of his colleagues, he opened for himself avenues of criticism never possible under the old critic-performer apartheid.

Such was Woollcott's integrity, moreover, that, because of his friendships and his intimate knowledge of the theater, his judgments gained rather than lost favor with the public. To his readers, it was always plain that Woollcott reserved the right to judge adversely and even to insult his friends if need be—both of which he frequently did, sometimes as part of a social game and sometimes with unmistakable seriousness. This behavior was one of the fortunate paradoxes of his character that fitted him uniquely for the office he held. For other critics, who could not sustain a similar ambivalence in their personal relationships, it may have been best to remain aloof. But for Woollcott, criticism meant ardent personal involvement.

His capacity for drifting into close personal relationships with the great personalities of his time was the result of his genuine liking for people of intelligence and wit. This tendency was only one of the diversities of his character that made him extraordinarily facile in dealing with the swift-changing forms and types of dramatic entertainment and with the maze of cross-currents formed by radio, motion picture, vaudeville, and legitimate theater. He was at ease with the manifold thematic and technical relationships among drama, literature, and the other allied arts. Moreover, he understood conflicts between the arts and economic forces, and he was keenly aware of the widespread dimming of traditional values in the theatrical professions. All these things he regarded as the legitimate province of dramatic criticism. As both reviewer and critic, he addressed himself to them whenever he saw the need to do so.

II *First and Second Thoughts*

Though Woollcott's first impressions of a dramatic production were usually accurate and his commentary penetrating, he distrusted the hasty first nighter's review that he was forced to compose "in what little retrospect the first hour after the curtain affords."[3] He was painfully aware of the difference between mere reviewing and true dramatic criticism; and though few critics ever fully matched his capacity to compose fresh, entertaining, balanced, and illuminating reviews night after night, he knew that he could do his best work only by gaining time for mature reflection and for the exacting composition that he demanded of himself. Although he could not escape the reviewer's nightly chore, Woollcott began compensating for the hastiness of his reviews by using his Sunday column, "Second Thoughts on First Nights," as a medium for more legitimate, fully developed dramatic criticism.[4]

If at first he had expected to use his Sunday column as a forum for rectifying his spontaneous judgments and the frequently effusive quality of his nightly reviews, he in actual practice rarely resorted to "Second Thoughts on First Nights" as an opportunity to modify or retract his initial judgments. Far from considering his own first impressions as infallible, he did not hesitate to make amends for egregious errors in judgment whenever they arose—as he did "with ashes in his hair" after having declared that the Arthur Hopkins production of Maxim Gorki's *Night Lodging* was "murky and despondent."[5] After attending a later performance, he recorded in "Second Thoughts" an apology for his first review, saying that the play now seemed to him "a thing of extraordinary vitality, a thoughtful, suggestive, enriching, exultant play, superbly acted."[6] He indicated, however, that, in the four months since he had first seen the play, its acting and production had been altered and greatly improved.

But retractions of this type are rare in "Second Thoughts." Woollcott was more likely to use the column to amplify and defend assertions he had already made. When he first remarked of a dramatization of William Dean Howells' *Rise of Silas Lapham* that "it is only as a fleeting glance backward that the play and production have any interest for us,"[7] he bolstered this partially developed argument by adding in the next Sunday edition that "the clumsy, ramshackle play contrived by Lillian Sabine from the Howells masterpiece is so completely devoid of dramatic or any other value that fidelity to the original could be its only excuse for production."[8]

Except for scattered and sporadic references, such as this one to the *Rise of Silas Lapham*, along with summaries of the week's offerings and references to plays or performers in a historical or comparative context, "Second Thoughts on First Nights" had only peripheral connections with the daily reviewing columns. To Woollcott, the world of the theater abounded in fascinating critical problems that were apart from and that transcended the consideration of any single, current production. Therefore, "Second Thoughts" became a regular opportunity for Woollcott to explore the larger, more perennial, and more significant aspects of theatrical taste, trends, personalities, and general history.

III   *The Proper Role of the Drama Critic*

Much of the appeal of Woollcott's early journalistic criticism lay in his carefully cultivated personal tone, with which he offset and helped to make obsolete the elevated and pedantic tone of the older "school" of dramatic criticism. The deceptively relaxed and chatty surface of his style anticipated that of the gossip columnists who were soon to become notorious and influential all over the country;

and though Woollcott never descended to the gross tactics of the professional gossipmonger, he sought to personalize his columns as much as possible without compromising his own standards. He did not hesitate, for instance, to share with his readers his personal views about the proper functions of the drama critic; and as time went on, he more and more frequently addressed himself to the task of defining his own role as a critic and as a man of belles-lettres.

He was both amused and distressed by the stereotyped public notions of the "typical" drama critic, and he deplored the caricatures upon which fiction writers traded. In "Second Thoughts" of December 25, 1921, he described several characterizations of drama critics that had appeared in novels by Samuel Hopkins Adams and Booth Tarkington. Because of these examples, he concluded that the current drama critic was primarily portrayed in literature "as a sort of snarling jackal of the theatre, a vain and sometimes dangerous creature, who can be endured socially only with considerable effort." Woollcott was encouraged, however, by Tarkington's prefatory admission that "the theatre has been moving a long way toward truthfulness. That it has so moved must be acknowledged as due in no little part to the impulse of journalistic criticism." Even so, Woollcott's view of the critic's task was neither that of the fictional caricature nor that of Tarkington's crusader after truth. His was an eminently practical and unpretentious view that was consistently expressed in terms best exemplified by this passage from "Second Thoughts":

The dramatic critic's function is somewhat akin to that of the attendant at some Florentine Court whose uneasy business was to taste each dish before it was fed to any one that mattered. He is an ink-stained wretch invited to each new play and expected, in the little hour that is left him after the fall of the curtain, to transmit something of that play's flavor, to write with whatever of fond tribute, sharp invective or amiable badinage will best express it, a description of the play as performed, in terms of the impression it made upon himself. If he likes it or dislikes it, he may even have time for a brow-furrowing attempt to say why, from which attempts spring all the foolish charges that he brings some silly little foot-rule of his own into the theatre with which to measure severely all the plays exhibited to him.[9]

IV *Playwrights Good and Bad*

In Woollcott's prewar months as critic for the *Times*, the most significant playwrights that he mentioned in his columns were English, Irish, and Scottish veterans like George Bernard Shaw, John

Galsworthy, Lord Dunsany, and James M. Barrie, who were already established and whose plays would continue to appear in the Broadway theaters for a long time to come. But upon Woollcott's return to his post after the war, a fresh battery of British and Irish dramatists had made their debuts in American theaters. Most of them found their way immediately into Woollcott's columns, where those of special stature—W. Somerset Maugham, John Drinkwater, John Masefield, St. John Ervine, A. A. Milne—received the serious critical attention that Woollcott knew they deserved.

Virtually all of the American playwrights of the time appeared in "The Play" or "Second Thoughts"; and though their plays were generally less substantial than those of the best British dramatists, they were far more numerous, offering greater variety in form and quality. Late in 1920, Woollcott listed the following as the most promising American playwrights of the day (by which he seems to have meant those of the current season): Edward Sheldon, Eugene O'Neill, Clare Kummer, James Forbes, Augustus Thomas, Zoë Akins, George Cohan, A. F. Thomas, Rachel Crothers, Phillip Moeller, and Eugene Walter.[10] The appearance of comparatively obscure figures listed beside the names of Edward Sheldon, George Cohan, and Eugene O'Neill highlights the difficulties of making critical judgments that, in the confused welter of dramatic offerings during that fast-moving era of the theater, would hold up under the passage of time. Though Woollcott praised some mediocre plays, many of them were popular successes like Anne Nichols' "Abie's Irish Rose," and he rarely failed to recognize the true worth of those playwrights whose reputations have now survived the perspective of thirty years and more.

Woollcott was as quick to celebrate those "riches of meaning just a little way below the surface"[11] of Edna St. Vincent Millay's fantasy of war called *Aria Da Capo* as he was to glow with pleasure in saying after the first performance of A. A. Milne's *Mr. Pim Passes By* that the play is "rich . . . in its stock of that sly and quiet humor with which he [Milne] used to fill the little dialogues signed A. A. M. in bygone numbers of *Punch*."[12] Toward the plays of O'Neill, whose career was contemporaneous with Woollcott's and whose "apprenticeship" is generally considered to have ended with the production of *Beyond the Horizon* in 1920, Woollcott maintained an attitude of restrained enthusiasm; he praised him highly when praise seemed due, but he clearly indicated any descent from the quality of art that he continued to expect of O'Neill's high talent.

Always a banner bearer for the well-constructed one act play, Woollcott was among the most enthusiastic supporters of the Provincetown Players and their Macdougal Street theater, and he was convinced that O'Neill's early plays for this group were among his best. He compared *The Dreamy Kid* with Theodore Dreiser's "The Hand of the Potter" in its capacity to induce in the audience "complete sympathy and pity for a conventionally abhorrent character."[13] Upon seeing one of the first performances of *Exorcism*, he spoke of O'Neill's "surplus creative energy which enables him, after the essential structure of the play has been attended to, to people it with original and distinctive characters, brought into the theatre with the breath of life in them and backgrounds that ask no aid from the man with the brush." In the same context he cited both *Bound East for Cardiff* and *Beyond the Horizon* as evidence that "as more and more of his plays have come to light, the mere abundance of this extra energy grows more interesting."[14]

Yet Woollcott slashed unmercifully at the dramatic structure of *Anna Christie* by describing it as clumsy and awkward and as "cluttered up with the rubbish of an earlier play from the wreckage of which O'Neill built this one." That play, Woollcott continued, succeeds in the theater despite its faulty structure by emerging as a memorable experience mostly "because it is crowded with life, because it has sprung from as fine an imagination as ever worked in our theatre, and because it has been wrought by a master of dramatic dialogue."[15] At the same time, he refused to limit the proper measure of O'Neill's talent to comparisons with current Broadway offerings. He demanded instead that *Anna Christie* maintain the standards already established by the playwright's previous work—a standard that was, by implication, unique to O'Neill.[16]

Woollcott had been too early and too keenly disillusioned by the commercialism of the professional theater to accept the common level of dramatic entertainments as the measure of any playwright whose work approached that of real genius. From time to time, when he was nettled beyond endurance by the sameness of the second rate offerings that were endlessly foisted upon the public, he burst into indictments of "stencil farces" or similarly stereotyped forms of entertainment:

A theatrical season is not considered complete unless it can boast from fifteen to twenty of those farces which involve a good deal of getting into the wrong bedroom and considerable screaming about it, together with a liberal

supply of honeymoon jokes and quite a lot of marital jealousy. It is considered best to unfold them in country houses or boats so that there will be
plenty of doors to bang. There can be short, agonized cries of "Dearest, you
don't understand," and "Darling, if you would only let me explain," with
the explanations themselves carefully postponed until it is 11 o'clock and
time for the suburbanites to start home.[17]

Or he devoted most of his Sunday page to delighted speculations
that the inviolable principle of the happy ending seemed to be
fading in the wake of several "hit plays"—including three of
O'Neill's—that had not bowed to the conventional "rule that a play
must end merrily and, if possible, connubially."[18] Similarly, he
railed against the virtually institutionalized practice of "custom
playwriting," observing of one play that, if it "was not written to
order for Miss Claire, it was probably rewritten for her, and if it was
not altered to fit, it looks as though it were."[19]

Despite Woollcott's abiding impulse to enjoy the theater and to
praise it whenever possible, or at very least to balance his reactions,
crass stupidities and violations of taste in playwriting summoned up
from the dark side of his critical self outbursts of condemnation that
more than justified his being considered one of the "Three Fat
Fates" of Broadway.[20] Indeed, theater people came to fear the quick
slash of his phraseology more than the displeasure of any other critic
in New York—not because it was necessarily more damaging
overtly, but because it was usually justifiable condemnation and
because it so thoroughly destroyed those precious personal
things—vanities and pretensions.

"A heavy-handed, tasteless and uncommonly oratorical play,"[21]
Woollcott said of one production; and of Percy Mackaye's *George
Washington* he remarked that the whole play was "an amorphous
thing, suitable perhaps for open air festivals or some patriotic
pageant, but absurd and futile in the theatre."[22] Offended by the
obvious misuse of the stage in John Drinkwater's historical dramatization of Mary Stuart, Woollcott reported to his readers that the
play itself proceeded only "after a singularly clumsy and rather fatuous prologue in which, from an all-engulfing darkness, the author
keeps piping the moral of the impending drama, a good deal in the
manner of a stereopticon lecturer taking aim with his pointer."[23]
Now and again, at moments when he found a play so badly conceived or so unoriginal as to seem altogether hopeless, his column
oozed his own peculiar verbal acid—as when he remarked of a lady

playwright that her play had "one of those leaky plots which proceed on their way only through a certain feeble-mindedness on the part of her characters,"[24] or when he observed of a current farce by a male playwright that it "has all the freshness of an eight-year-old newspaper which had been used as a shelf-covering in a long-locked closet."[25]

If a play happened to be bad enough, Woollcott might eventually address himself to it in both his daily and his Sunday columns, and thereby make the production such a *cause célèbre* that it might be nominated as one of Woollcott's choices for the ten worst plays of the season. This fate befell the ill-written and worse-managed attempt to make dramatic entertainment of the stories and poems of Edgar Allan Poe in the spring of 1920. The show was billed as the *Poe Playlets;* and when Woollcott first saw them, he unequivocally despatched them by simply branding them "the lowest ebb in the playgoing experience of this reviewer."[26] Shortly afterward, having included the adaptation among the ten worst plays, he tried to give his readers some idea why the production had represented such a low point in his experience. At one point in the playlet *Lenore,* he explained, the character representing Poe told his critically ill wife that *Blackwood's* had just refused his story "The Gold Bug," whereupon she asked that he cheer her up by reciting "The Raven." The actor obliged with an incredibly strained and overdramatized recitation, and Mrs. Poe shortly thereafter expired. "The audience was not taken by surprise," observed Woollcott. "It was not feeling any too well, either."[27]

V *Dramatic Translation and Adaptation*

As a deplorable attempt to create a play by using the materials of another literary form or medium, the *Poe Playlets* represent one of those theatrical phenomena that invariably outraged Woollcott's sense of propriety. If he found what he considered a good translation or adaptation, he was pleased and judged the merits of the whole production. But when the transposition of materials was badly done, as it usually was, he wrote of it as part of his unflagging campaign against the widespread abuse of literary sources and models. Early in his career, as has been noted, Woollcott had inadvertently created wide publicity for his displeasure with bad German translations when he wrote his hasty review of *Taking Chances;* but he repeatedly returned to the problem in his criticism, especially with regard to the prolific spawn of translations from the French.

Of one translation, *Kiki*, Woollcott observed that David Belasco had "landed (somewhat heavily) on the expedient of writing it all out in the argot of an American chorus girl, with just a *soupçon* of French words and gestures."[28] In this respect, Woollcott's most forceful complaint took the form of an essay entitled "The Terrible Translation," which was eventually included in *Shouts and Murmurs* and which observes that translators tend to be "either men who cannot read French or who cannot write English. They achieve either a weird jargon that is half Harlem and half Montparnasse or they turn all the speeches into an Ollendorf idiom the like of which never found voice on land or sea. The heroines of such hybrids are given either to remarks like this: 'Cheese it! Voilà le policeman!' or to remarks like this: 'Is it not necessary that the aunt of my friend assist'?"[29] In all fairness to English translators, however, Woollcott made clear that "our mauling of French scripts is not a patch on what the French adaptors have done to English and American plays. It is a reasonably safe wager that 'Peg de mon Coeur' was frequently weird."[30]

With almost equal intensity he despised unsuccessful attempts to make plays out of novels. Sensitive to the unique properties of the two separate literary forms, he was incensed at the mauling of a good novel but pleased with a good adaptation. Early in his career as critic, he was thrilled by the reappearance of William Gillette in the theater version of A. Conan Doyle's Sherlock Holmes stories, which had first been dramatized in the 1890s, and he defended the sheer theatricalism of that adaptation.[31] But only a week later he wrote somewhat fretfully about Ethel Barrymore's return to Broadway as Mrs. McChesney in Edna Ferber's rather "gawky and incoherent" dramatization of her own short stories about Mrs. McChesney. Woollcott found himself publicly lamenting the misfortune that Miss Ferber had not been able to make of her own excellent fiction a play that could stand comparison with the dramatized versions of the Chimmie Fadden stories, the Sherlock Holmes stories, or Irvin S. Cobb's Judge Priest stories.[32]

Particularly sceptical of fiction writers who tried to make plays of their own stories, he was surprised and somewhat relieved whenever he could speak approvingly of such transmutations. He was pleased to give Mary Roberts Rinehart a good review for her dramatic thriller *The Bat*, and he was even more pleased to be able to indicate to his readers that, despite the playwright's deliberate silence on the matter, the play was really only a well-dramatized treatment of her own novel *The Circular Staircase*. Moreover, Woollcott suggested that the adaptation was so subtle as to have gone over the heads of many first nighters who had not rightly perceived Rinehart's real purpose in mixing low comedy with mystery. "Not real thrills," contended Woollcott, "but a state of bogus, self-conscious excitement—that is her game."[33] Unfortunately, Woollcott could not have so much fun with most similar adaptations; and when Zona Gale came to Broadway with a dramatized version of her best-known novel *Miss Lulu Bett*, the *Times* critic was minded once again to quote "the ancient pronunciamento that somehow novelists cannot write for the stage, that good books do not make good plays, &c., &c.—all old rubber stamps of dramatic criticism, which you are just about to discard as worn out when along comes a play like 'Miss Lulu Bett' and makes them indispensable."[34]

Rarely did he misjudge the potential longevity of a well-translated, capably produced foreign play of real excellence, even though in theme or structure it might represent a departure from accepted American standards. To his mind, for instance, the American premiere of Ferenc Molnar's *Liliom* ended the Theater Guild season of 1920–1921 "in a blaze of glory," even if it was "a piece most painful to Pharisees, for it walks in arm-on-shoulder comradeship with publicans and sinners."[35] Later, when he devoted most of his Sunday page to this play, he gave his readers a resumé of the action, a short history of its genesis and composition, and a complimentary description of Lee Simonson's mounting of the production. But he condemned Eva Le Gallienne's acting because, instead of playing a peasant, she was "an actress whose playing is just a little pinched and pursed and one whose speech is incorrigibly elegant to the last."[36]

VI *The Intractable Dramatists*

For those English, Scotch, and Irish playwrights who, even in Woollcott's day, were already becoming near classic figures in modern theatrical history, Woollcott maintained attitudes that ranged from adulation to guarded optimistic concern. He was altogether charmed by J. M. Barrie and his plays, a subject upon which he was to write one of his best short essays. For the Irish Players and their principal figures—J. M. Synge, W. B. Yeats, Lady Gregory—he had great respect even though their real influence as a group or

movement seemed to have passed. Whenever he saw a good production of anything by Gilbert and Sullivan, he seemed so refreshed
that he wrote of them with special verve and warmth.

At this point in Woollcott's career, George Bernard Shaw had
risen through a series of tempestuous controversies to become
widely accepted as "the world's greatest contemporary dramatist."[37]
By 1920, the Theater Guild had virtually adopted his plays for their
American production; and despite an earlier wave of American out-
rage against such matters as the immorality of *Mrs. Warren's Profession*, Shaw was one of Broadway's most reliable if most constantly
provocative playwrights. In reviewing the regular succession of
Shaw's plays on which the guild repeatedly pinned its hopes during
the early 1920s, Woollcott was inclined to maintain a curiously ambivalent attitude—curious, at least, for a critic whose value judgments were usually clearly defined and unwavering.

One of his early articles in the *Times* was a dissertation with the
indicative title "The Dramatist Intractable" which used Shaw as a
prime instance of the playwright who demands and gets almost
anything he requires of producers and directors, including his own
choice of the individual star to play his leading role. This part the
playwright has, in fact, frequently created for an actor or actress,
just as Shaw had written the leading role in *Major Barbara* expressly
for Eleanor Robson. Preparing to use Shaw as an example of "the
grandeur of the modern playwright," Woollcott made this general
observation: "The popular notion of the playwright as a humble
fellow, standing meek in the manager's outer office, is food for a
producer's melancholy laughter. Your genuine dramatist, unless he
be hungry, is haughty. He has the manners of a magnate, and the
managers speak him soft."[38]

Aside from disapproving the power base from which Shaw operated, Woollcott also distrusted the almost purely intellectual appeal
of Shaw's plays. Even when he was inclined to like a Shaw play, as
he did *Heartbreak House*, Woollcott usually avoided a discussion of
its intellectual content by dealing with it in terms of its author
striving to account for it as another manifestation of Shaw's icono-
clastic wit. "In its graver moments," said Woollcott of *Heartbreak
House*, "the more familiar mood of Shavian exasperation gives way
to accents akin to Cassandra's" yet because "it is always possible to
find the clear, honest eyes of Bernard Shaw peering out from behind
the thin disguise of one of his characters,"[39] it is always plain that

the author is speaking the moral of the piece—which, in the case of *Heartbreak House,* is "the challenge that no people can afford to create leisure if that leisure is to be wasted in fruitless and unsocial idleness."[40]

In the long run, Woollcott refused to believe that Shaw's intellectual adventures in playwriting had the kind of universality that would survive. When Woollcott was pressed to the wall by outraged public responses to his contention that Barrie's plays would enjoy greater longevity than Shaw's (especially Barrie's *Peter Pan,* whose theatrical permanence he predicted in Chapter VIII of *Shouts and Murmurs),* he would not retreat. Instead, he bolstered his original argument with the following surmise: "that never, not even in 'Candida' has Shaw given to the theatre anything which has the universality in time of 'Peter Pan' or 'Mary Rose'; that reviving most of Shaw's old plays is a little like fighting in last year's trenches; that the journalistic element in all Shaw's work, while endowing it with much of its present force and value and significance, at the same time dooms it to grow stale like the headlines of yesteryear."[41]

VII *Players and Their Playing*

It is a clue to Woollcott's sympathy with performers that in 1915 he was mildly annoyed with Ethel Barrymore's decision to return to the Broadway stage as Mrs. McChesney. He was fretful not only because Ferber's adaptation did not strike him as worthy at any time of Miss Barrymore's talents, but especially because at this particular time a star was relying upon such a play to help reestablish her after a considerable absence from the Broadway theaters. Nonetheless, Woollcott rarely thought that the star of a Broadway show was properly cast in a part or even in a play that was commensurate with the star's highest talents. Either a mediocre performer tended to be thrust into a role perceptibly beyond his capacities or a high-powered performer was too frequently asked to "carry" a weak play. The moment Woollcott spotted one of these mismatchings, the machinery that operated his sense of taste and proportion shifted into gear, and he then did his best to separate all the weak elements from the strong ones and to assign whatever praise or blame seemed warranted. In any instance of gross mismatching of a player and a play, however, his sympathies were most likely to be with the player; and upon those uncommon occasions when a good cast and a good play seemed equally made for each other, he would be so comprehensively happy that he might call upon his most expansive phrase of celebration—that there was "dancing in the streets."

Woollcott's undisguised admiration of certain stars is obvious everywhere in his criticism; and though his close friendship with many of them was genuine and was founded upon mutual interests and true compatibility, he seemed nonetheless flattered by their willingness to accept him as an intimate. His near adulation of Mrs. Fiske as both actress and woman is unmistakable in every line he wrote about her, and especially in the book that he based upon his interviews with her. If he sometimes found fault with the work of the Barrymores, he felt himself more than their casual acquaintance, and he persistently trumpeted their stature as the foremost family of the American theater. During the flourishing years of the Algonquin Wits, he became a kind of sponsor for such unmistakably talented young actresses as Margalo Gillmore and Ruth Gordon, with both of whom he remained close friends to the end of his days. In the middle and later years of his career, his letters and his public writings are full of choice personal memorabilia concerning these celebrities, as well as his cherished companions Harpo Marx, Noel Coward, and Alfred Lunt and Lynn Fontanne. As personal but passing acquaintances, he numbered dozens of performers who were interesting and important in every kind of entertainment, from vaudeville and musical comedy to revivals of Shakespeare and the Classical Greek.

Apart from Woollcott's fascination with individual performers, he had an abiding interest in considering the place of the actor in the theater and in defining that unique theatrical institution known as "stardom." He had little sympathy with those critics who considered the actor "a mere annoyance, to be tolerated a little while longer until we can all think up some less disgusting instrument for transmitting the playwright's thoughts to the public."[42] In 1919, he offered his own definition of a star as "a player of such quality that he can greatly enrich any reasonably suitable play . . . , and also of such reputation that the very appearance of his name in the bills is sufficient to draw a considerable following, regardless of what the play may chance to be."[43] To Woollcott's mind, no producer or director could create a true star by means of advertising or by any other such artificial means;[44] for he believed true stardom to be of such slow growth that the highest ranks changed so infinitesimally that the stars of a decade ago continued to be the stars of the day and only a few new stars rose into the theatrical firmament at any given time. Moreover, this very slowness of evolution created stars of different "magnitudes"; only two or three stars attained the first magnitude for a measurable period of time; and their rise was accompanied by about the same number of the second magnitude. All lesser stars remained scattered below.

One of Woollcott's most interesting theories, a notion that he held tenaciously and defended frequently, is that the highest talent for acting is the product of both heritage and training, though heritage is by far the most important requirement of the two. "It took several generations of the stage to launch Gilda Varesi," he once said in a short biographical sketch of the current star of Varesi's *Enter Madame*, "and she went to the best dramatic school of our time. She played with Mrs. Fiske."[45] Later he included in one of his books a short historical essay in which he traces the dominating influence of the great American acting families upon the development of the American theater. Here he felt justified in arguing that there is no other art "in which the force of heredity seems to play so controlling a part."[46] He suggests, too, that an essay upon the hereditary talent of playwrights could well arise from his observation that five of the ten best plays of the 1920–1921 season were written by "persons born in the theatre."[47]

During his years on the *Times*, Woollcott developed and refined his methods of conveying to his readers the essential qualities of any performer's work; and though his comments frequently said as much about himself as about the actor, the results were that he soon became known as one of the liveliest phrasemakers of his day. In his prewar years he was eloquent in praise of John Barrymore's power as a Shakespearean actor, and he defended the "natural" acting of John Drew against charges that Drew was always the same, whatever role he was performing. Woollcott's excessive enthusiasm for the histrionic talent of one Jacob Ben-Ami seemed almost ridiculous to some of his colleagues, but in most cases his open and honest enjoyment of good acting was infectious to his readers.

At the age of nineteen, Helen Hayes caught his eye when she was playing the title role in *Bab;* and the soundness of his immediate enthusiasm for her "flawless precision of playing"[48] has been borne out by Miss Hayes' fifty years as a star of the first magnitude. He spoke also of "the splendor of Miss Anglin, the lovely music of her voice and the prodigious, the amazing energy that is hers and hers alone."[49] He was enthralled by the "witchery" of Jeanne Eagels,[50] and in an excess of nostalgia he threatened to grow "incoherent" in praising Elsie Janis as "the best music hall artist of them all."[51] Lionel Atwill's role as Deburau he called "a performance of distinguished beauty, one full to the brim of charm and eloquence and understanding."[52] As for the prolific part playing of Walter Hampden, he sometimes had the highest praise and sometimes the keenest derision; for his comments depended upon the widely variable quality of Hampden's acting from role to role.[53]

To the various newspapers whose circulation his columns boosted, and to the theater companies whose audiences bought tickets in response to his lively commentary, Woollcott's ebullience was of inestimable value; but to the acting profession he was best known and most widely feared as the critic whose phrases could cut nearest the bone and who could, in fact, mortally wound the inept or unlucky actor, whether the artist was an established star or the merest minion in a cast.[54] The following excerpts from his columns indicate something of the airy and almost cavalier fashion in which he could despatch a bad job of acting: "One could wish that Mrs. Lincoln would at least sound like an American";[55] "[Nance O'Neill] sits still and gazes upon Esteban, but spiritually she has gone out for a brief rest in the wings";[56] "Mr. Blair is no comedian. He has been many things on the stage in his day, but he has never been funny";[57] "[*Thy Name Is Woman*] is played with the blacksmith touch, most of it driven home in a manner that insultingly assumes something less than the decent minimum of intelligence in the expectant audience across the footlights";[58] "[Leslie Howard] indulges in the most extraordinary clowning, expressing mild surprise by almost falling down and the slightest embarrassment by something strongly resembling convulsions."[59]

Nor did the producers, directors, and technicians escape unscathed. Of a production of Euripides' *Iphigenia in Aulis* he observed that "Mr. Browne's way of bedizening and prettifying these austere Greek tragedies is nothing short of an abomination. He fills his stage with a weaving and writhing Delsartian chorus that is like festooning a severe Greek temple with pink cheesecloth."[60] With regard to the misguided efforts of a sound effects man in another production, he remarked that "*The Six-Fifty* is the dramatization of a train wreck, accomplished off-stage at the Hudson and sounding a good deal like someone throwing a fit in a junk pile."[61] Moreover,

Woollcott had a disconcerting way of seeing through the inept ploys of directors who attempted to fool audiences into accepting transparent stage tricks or awkwardly doctored manuscripts, as when he said of *Smiling Through:* "Very likely it was necessary to have Miss Cowl play both the Moonyeen Clare of long ago and the Kathleen—but this necessity leads to one of those trick performances in which, no matter how plausibly the player leaves the scene, the wily audience says: 'Ah, ha! She has gone to change her clothes and come back as the other one.' "[62] In another instance, he could not resist using an egregious pun to expose the excessive cutting of Portia's part in *The Merchant of Venice*—a deliberate cutting that had been done to emphasize the role of Shylock, played by an indifferent actor named Edward Vroom. The cuts were "made this time, the wags said, to leave plenty of Vroom at the top."[63]

Woollcott's playgoing had not given him reason to place great trust in the general taste and competence of American producers, especially with regard to their treatment, as already noted, of some of the foreign and classic playwrights. He was, in fact, almost bitter about the American production of Ibsen's plays; for he charged that "no playwright, living or dead, has suffered such shoddy and generally incompetent production in this century as poor Henrik Ibsen and it is really astonishing that the notion that he could write good plays has nevertheless survived to this day."[64]

VIII *Constructive Criticism*

It is grossly unfair to Woollcott, however, to assume, as some people have done, that he was capable of nothing more than an infectious but childlike effusiveness at one extreme or of a sometimes petulant and sometimes casually vicious destructiveness at the other. Actually, his columns frequently offered constructive criticism of the most sensible and valuable kind. That the American theater has failed to heed so many of his suggestions has been more to its loss than to its credit. As many of his essays and articles show, he shared with Mrs. Fiske the conviction that the repertory system was not good for the American theater, and he did all he could to explain and defend the alternatives. Since he was also convinced that the most serious weakness of the American stage was its obvious lack of gifted directors, he continued to urge that the profession should remedy the deficiency. When he saw the first efforts of Guthrie McClintic as director of Milne's *Dover Road*, he announced that, "as the American theatre's poverty is most conspicuous in the matter of directors, his [McClintic's] advent takes on the nature of an occasion."[65]

Part of the remedy for the most palpable weaknesses of the theater, he felt, was the encouragement of high-quality experimental theaters on the professional level, as best exemplified by the Washington Square Players—though he warned against the prevailing tendency to rely upon theater buildings that were too small to afford audiences an adequate sense of their own reaction and interaction during performances. With regard to the audiences themselves, he nursed a conviction that the physical peculiarities of each theater attract a special audience that should be cultivated by the theater management. "It is the business of every faithful playgoer," he announced during his first years as critic, "to help each theatre find its own particular audience: it is entirely the theatre's business to keep it when found."[66]

One of Woollcott's loftiest proposals was that those who were always offering to "endow" the theater should give at least one leading producer his total independence to produce whatever plays he liked in whatever fashion he liked, without any threat of commercial failure or the destructive wrath of audiences, critics, or society in general. His insistence upon the necessity for the theater to be free was a recurring theme in Woollcott's criticism.[67]

His abiding wish to help the theater change in useful ways is reflected not only in large and lofty matters but in small things as well. Since he regularly kept notes to himself in the form of queries, he set out from time to time to answer these "scattered notes on unimportant little flaws" that, if brought together, "should be suggestive, helpful and doubtless constitute that mysterious thing people have in mind when (usually in a moment of acute irritation) they talk about 'constructive criticism.' "[68] In this instance, his notes included queries—mostly framed as rhetorical questions— concerning faulty pronunciation, senseless cutting of script, nonsensical lyrics, anachronistic costuming, miscasting, and trite dialogue. In the same spirit, he did not hesitate to suggest to the actors in Shaw's *Heartbreak House* that "a mumbled scene may save time, but it is the last device in the world to ward off boredom."[69] Also, tired of actors who simply copied traditional interpretations of classic roles, he sometimes suggested fresh approaches, as when he pointed out that critical accolades might await that actor who would be willing to interpret the usually overbearing character of Pe-

truchio in Shakespeare's *The Taming of the Shrew* as "a philosophi-
cal, mild-mannered fellow, who has read in a book somewhere that
shrews can be roared, starved, and terrorized into docility."[70]

IX Shouts and Murmurs

Despite the only modest commercial success of his earliest anthologies, Woollcott felt by the summer of 1921 that the best of his
contributions to "The Play" and "Second Thoughts," as well as some
of his earliest magazine sketches about theatrical subjects, might be
successfully recycled. Under the title *Shouts and Murmurs*, this
compilation reached the bookshops early in 1922; but, drawing upon
his unique and extensive inventory of theatrical lore, he had
selected a title so ingenious, and so appropriate to the contents, that
he used it again for similar purposes. It was a phrase from a "stage
anecdote" so venerable and so obscure of origin that Woollcott's
Foreword presents as an "Old Fable" what is really a short parable—the kind of tale that, in later years, he liked to tell or retell, or
to create somehow out of materials otherwise barren of tale-telling
potential. This tiny "fable"—about the old actor at the Players' Club
who, having impressed the circle with his long experience at Drury
Lane, at last discloses with pride that he had always done the
offstage noises and was therefore officially listed on the programs as
"Shouts and Murmurs"—sets the tone for the whole collection.

Indeed, the pieces that appear in *Shouts and Murmurs* are unsur-
passed in the long tradition of the stage anecdote. As ancient as the
stage itself, this highly esoteric and largely oral kind of anecdote had
awaited only a professional writer who was saturated with stage lore
and who had a flair for developing anecdotes into full-blown tales.
No other writer in the history of the American theater, perhaps in
the history of any theater, was better equipped than Woollcott to
make this traditionally oral and esoteric kind of tale both permanent
and popular. In *Shouts and Murmurs*, as well as later in *Enchanted
Aisles* and *Going to Pieces*, and in the "Program Notes" of *While
Rome Burns* and *Long, Long, Ago*, Woollcott came very close to
making the stage anecdote a distinctive literary type, one that appeals to the general reader but was previously reserved for the ini-
tiated.

Woollcott launches his anthology with a set of three short
sketches, each celebrating a crucial but obscure episode in the
career of a theater celebrity. All three are introduced by the chapter
heading "Behind the Scenes," wherein he creates a tissue of sharply

etched images that highlight the contrasts between the glorified, make–believe world of the play and the real backstage world of "darkness and ropes and strange fusty smells." His intention, he says, is not to disillusion the reader by taking him on "an actual journey backstage" but to heighten his pleasure by making "an excursion among the circumstances which have made plays what they are."

The opening sketch, "An Emergency Masterpiece," is an account of the way in which Frank Craven's *The First Year*, a fresh but unpretentious comedy dramatizing the hazards of the first year of marriage, had reached Broadway and had become a success even though it was "the nervous rush work of an actor frankly in need of a job." Craven, descendant of an old theater family and accustomed from childhood to playing "turkey dates" for meals on holidays, but reared as a boarder on a farm during his schooldays, had inherited "all the conditions which make (and always have made) for good work in the theater." The punchline of this sketch is a good example of what might be called "the celestial touch" in Woollcott's writing. A few months before Craven had made his first hit as an actor in 1911, his mother, in her last illness, had looked down from her apartment window and had said to her son of the new theater nearly built below, "You might play there sometime." And in fact, while waiting for his curtain calls in *Bought and Paid For* at the new playhouse, Craven had stepped outside and blown a kiss at the darkened windows where his actress-mother had died. Then he "started for the scene that was to lift him to the stars."

The other two pieces in this opening chapter are "O. Henry, Playwright," and "The Shadow on a Great Success." The first, a choice revelation of a little-known side of William Sydney Porter's career, tells of George Tyler's attempts to commission the writing of a play by the famous short story writer; of Porter's frantic correspondence, promising the script, pleading for an advance, and offering all his dramatic royalty rights in return; and of his receiving the money and arriving in New York, his Bagdad, where he immediately "drifted happily off among the bazaars"—and never wrote his comedy. The third and closing sketch is a kind of lament that the hit play *Enter Madame*, written and acted by Gilda Varesi as a tribute to her famous prima donna mother, was produced too late for that lustrous and temperamental opera star to share in its triumph. Incidentally, this little piece also tells how Gilda Varesi rose to stardom by being "the most destructive understudy in the

American theater," for she always managed to get the role she understudied.

Chapter II is another package of three small sketches under the title "The Knock at the Stage Door," each concerned with one or another of the ways by which people contrive to get into the world of the theater. "Born of Strolling Players" (the opening phrase of Eleanora Duse's note in *Who's Who in the Theatre*) is another of Woollcott's arguments that the common denominator among great performers is that most of them are born into theater families. Here he remembers that the young Margalo Gillmore, who had reminded critics of Ethel Barrymore, had shared with her a distinguished theater ancestry—as had Mrs. Fiske, Julia Marlowe, Laurette Taylor, and the other great theater families like the Booths, the Jeffersons, the Kembles, the Terrys, the Drews. Loaded with anecdotes to prove that historically the stage had long been "a world apart," the sketch reminds all casual stage aspirants that, while showfolk children are growing up in the theater, others not so privileged "not only [are] not learning how to act, but, by every experience and precept and taboo of the breakfast table and the sidewalk and the schoolyard, are busily learning not to act at all."

The small piece "The Swarming Amateurs" pursues this theme by turning to the rapid rise of amateur theatricals in the hinterlands, where, by the early 1920s, the professional theater had "left the citizens to darkness and the movies." The result was that plays in print (like O'Neill's and even Susan Glaspell's) had become more widely known among amateurs than among professionals in New York, and the professionals had begun to fear that the amateurs might ruin the profession. In "Dr. Gundelfinger," however, Woollcott argues that the real danger with amateurs in the theater is that "men who would never think of attempting a novel or an ode or even a book of essays are not one whit abashed at writing a four-act problem play." Citing incidents of manuscripts written by streetcar conductors, inmates of mental hospitals, and obsessed surgeons, Woollcott offers as his candidate for "the most unbelievable play" an effort sent him in all seriousness by one Professor Gundelfinger, from which he quotes passages of the most incredible dialogue. He concludes that the sickness of the amateur playwright is that he tries to write plays without knowing anything at all about the theater.

"Gunpowder Plots" is Woollcott's half-frivolous complaint against the overuse of stage gunfire as one of the "mean devices" to "unnerve the audience." Resenting this ploy as "like cheating at solitaire," he points out that really good playwrights like Frank Craven manage to get equally strong effects by quieter and more legitimate means "than do the bullying melodramatists with whole arsenals at their disposal." In murder plays, therefore, Woollcott prefers "a knife stuck quietly and modestly between the ribs," and he gains pleasure for similar reasons from remembering the ways in which gunplay has gone wrong in crucial scenes by forcing actors into all sorts of impromptu stage business and desperate ad-libbing, of which he relates several classic instances. Though he mentions specifically a half-dozen other stage devices of which he is weary, he threatens to ask the secretary of state to disarm the drama.

But he is also tired of some of the outworn devices of the drama critics; and he protests in "Capsule Criticism" the unvarying use of such terms as "adequate" and "treading the boards." Above all, he regrets the verbosity and prolixity of dramatic criticism as a genre. Providing a short history of the "thousand word" tradition among famous critics, he argues that "the most telling of all dramatic criticisms have found expression in less than fifty words" and that the best of these "capsule criticisms" have probably been oral ones. The body of the essay is an entertaining and comprehensive marshaling of stage anecdotes, related as backgrounds for both classic and little-known "capsule criticisms." Among the "headlines," for example, is John Palmer's "Shylock as Mr. Tree"; among the reviews is Eugene Field's "Mr. [Creston] Clarke played the King [Lear] all evening as though under constant fear that some one else was going to play the Ace"; and among the oral ones is Beerbohm Tree's classic plea to the ladies in waiting at a rehearsal of Henry VIII: "Just a little more virginity, if you don't mind." To Woollcott, all these statements are superior examples of what, earlier in the essay, he had called "the happy sentence that speaks volumes."

"Another Foreign Author," an entertaining and important document in theater history, is ostensibly an essay upon the contemporary status of Shakespeare in the American theater; but it is more directly a carefully argued, cleverly written treatise about the ways in which the advent of Naturalistic drama had made the production of Shakespeare almost impossible in the early twentieth century. Shakespeare, he contends, has not been so much "neglected" as replaced by something altogether different: "The best plays of today differ from Shakespeare's as sharply as his own differed from the deathless tragedies which were written on the shores of the Aegean when all the world was young." After remarking briefly on "the circumstances which Ibsen helped mightily to create," Woollcott as a conclusion declares, "the imagination is subvened in the playhouse today. It has been pampered and Shakspere [*sic*] is a strain upon it."

If "Another Foreign Author" is a historical essay presented as a rumination upon Shakespeare, "The Celebrated Decline of the Drama" is a rumination, presented as a historical essay, about Mrs. Mowatt's *Fashion*. Woollcott begins with the argument that critics Nathan, Winter, Brander Matthews, and George Henry Lewes had all shared the idea behind the "antiphonal chant" of Mr. and Mrs. Curdle in Charles Dickens' *Nicholas Nickleby* that "The Drama is gone, perfectly gone"; but Woollcott's argument focuses thereafter upon Mrs. Mowatt and her early comedy and upon Poe's review of it in *The Broadway Journal* in 1845. Even then, it seems, the critics were crying that the drama was declining, as Poe cried when he charged that *Fashion* was only an inadequate latter-day imitation of *The School for Scandal*, without "originality or invention." Yet, Woollcott points out, "how great would have been his [Poe's] pain and surprise could he have foreseen that the imitative 'Fashion' would itself become the immediate forerunner and model for many and many a play."

In Chapter XI of *Shouts and Murmurs*, which consists of short, pithy reviews of three O'Neill plays, Woollcott once again uses in a general introduction the emergence of an important theater artist to advance his theory that the surest way to success in the theater is to be born into it. Here, however, Woollcott makes it clearer than ever that a playwright born of show folks, as O'Neill was, must also get far away from the theater during his formative years, in order to know the real world, as O'Neill had done when he roamed the seas as a youth, creating for himself a "little legend of wildness." These two biographical factors, insists Woollcott, are the very ones that, "under the doctrine of chances, one would rather expect to find present in the equipment of the Great American Playwright."

In his review of *Beyond the Horizon*, Woollcott declares that O'Neill's first long play, written after a succession of his one acts had been produced in experimental theaters, is a play that despite "its looseness and a certain high-and-mighty impracticability, was possessed of elements of greatness." The greatness, it seemed to Woollcott, came from O'Neill's knowledge of people and from the

sureness of his dramatic instinct. But its impracticability—the unnecessary splitting of all scenes into both interiors and exteriors, for
instance—bespoke the inexperience of the playwright who does not
yet know that "in the theater what you want and what you get are
very different." This particular ineptitude seems to have di-
minished, however, in *The Emperor Jones*, wherein "the as yet
unbridled Eugene O'Neill" managed to weave "a most potent spell,
thanks partly to the force and cunning of its author, thanks partly to
the admirable playing of Charles S. Gilpin in a title rôle so predomi-
nant that the play is little more than a dramatic monologue." Although mostly a graphic recounting of the action, this review manages to make an important ethnic observation: that until *The Emperor Jones*, the American drama had created "no first rate play
which has a negro rôle of Gilpin's stature," and especially no such
role actually to be played by a Negro, as Gilpin was.

And in the third O'Neill review, that of *The Hairy Ape*, "a brutal,
startling, dismaying, and singularly vivid play," Woollcott concludes
his tracing of O'Neill's development from the impractical playwright
of *Beyond the Horizon* to one whose "new play suggested a greater
familiarity with the theater as an instrument." Disclosing that the
original of Yank was a huge Irish stoker whom O'Neill had known at
sea, Woollcott vividly narrates the action, defends the play against
charges that the "fantastic" element is too long delayed, and partially agrees with fellow critics that Yank's necessarily profane language is "inadequate"; but he contends that a more legitimate criticism might be leveled at the language of the society people, which
"suggests too much the way the duchesses talk in a scullery-maid's
first novel."

Of all the pieces in *Shouts and Murmurs*, none is more completely a product of the theater than "Deburau, Pere, and Guitry,
Fils." It is not only an essay written by a drama critic about a play,
its author, and its star, but the playwright was also "an actor and the
son of a greater one," and the play is based upon the career of a great
performer who is replaced by his son. The play is Sacha Guitry's
Deburau, "a lonely and beautiful play which is an expression of the
philosophy of the stage, the credo of the actor, the sad-faced comedian's *apologia pro vita sua*"; and its star was Lionel Atwill in his
debut. Even though the essay is both a historical sketch and an
act-by-act review of the play, it emerges as a kind of rhapsody about
the famous personages who "come to life in its scenes." More than
anything else, Woollcott rhapsodizes about Guitry's sensitive dra-

matic treatment of the elder Deburau, the immortal Pierrot of the Theatre des Funambules in Paris, who according to legend knew and loved Marie Duplessis—the even more legendary "Lady of the Camellias," known through Dumas' play as "Camille"—and who in his last infirmity says his public farewell in matchless pantomime before passing the role of Pierrot to his son.

In Chapter XIV of *Shouts and Murmurs*, Woollcott's rhapsodies on *Deburau* and *Peter Pan* give way to "It was 'Trilby' "— Woollcott's celebration of his childhood favorite as book and play, best sellers both, though the "artlessly put together" play rode "like a cork on the wave" created by Du Maurier's novel. Woollcott's essay is a charming pastiche of anecdotes about the cast, the various revivals, the peculiarities of certain performances, and the many burlesques of *Trilby*.

"Palmy Days" is an account of the peculiar way in which Wilton Lackaye, the original Svengali in the *Trilby* play, parlayed an informal role as a "flowing-bearded lounger in a Western bar" into a full-blown role in a Western drama. The tradition of the "Western" prompts Woollcott to recall the triumphant California performances of Lotta Crabtree and the later Far West tours of Minnie Maddern Fiske, who followed "a trail which Lotta had blazed for her."

In "Mr. Tinney," Woollcott pays tribute to the last great performer to appear in *Shouts and Murmurs*, though Frank Tinney was a great performer only in a special sense—as the American vaudeville star who had "earned an income comparable to that of the President of the United States by the simple process of telling bad jokes as badly as possible."

The last two chapters of *Shouts and Murmurs* are closely related, but only one of them, "The Chauve-Souris," is an essay. The other chapter is a parodic playlet called "Zowie; or, the Curse of an Akins Heart," which Woollcott wrote for the single performance of a burlesque of the "Chauve-Souris" entertainments, whose history and character he describes in the essay. In 1922, the *Chauve-Souris*, a troupe of Russian vaudeville performers who had entertained at the Bat Restaurant in Moscow, reached Broadway via Paris and London. Because the group had arisen from the illustrious Moscow Art Theater,[71] the caliber of their acts was surprisingly high and the quality, at least to Woollcott, "baffling." One of the *Chauve-Souris* revues, for instance, was the precisionist musical routine called "The March of the Wooden Soldiers," whose music and color had captivated the sophisticates of the Algonquin Round Table.

Having perceived that great fun might come of their occupying an off night of the *Chauve-Souris* stage with some amateur variety acts of their own, The Vicious Circle invited friends to the Forty-ninth Street Theater and presented "No, Sirree," a burlesque version of the *Chauve-Souris*. The circle presentation included "takeoffs" of editorial policies, movies, American vaudeville, and the legitimate theater, and of plays by O'Neill, Milne, and Zoë Akins. Woollcott's "playlet" was a satire upon two plays by Akins. Jascha Heifetz played the offstage violin music, and an unexpected treat for everybody, one not listed on the program, was the first performance of Robert Benchley's now-famous "Treasurer's Report" which the author had sketched in desperation during his taxi ride to the theater.[72]

According to Woollcott's prefatory account in *Shouts and Murmurs*, the main reason for his travesty was that, after he had seen in a single season "two plays by Zoë Akins in each of which the heroine kept being ruined and ruined and ruined, this hitherto blameless chronicler of the theater momentarily lost control of himself, went mad, and wrote the following play." But the parody is more than his tongue-in-cheek explanation suggests. He loads it with the affected and outworn phrases that had grown stale on the programs of all the second rate, unoriginal shows he had seen. The play was a "romanza," taking place "in the heart of a great city" in the "printemps," and it was prefaced by a romantic but irrelevant quotation from "the Persian." Both the names of characters—"*Marmaduke La Salle*, a stomach specialist"; "*Zhoolie Venable*, a suppressed desire"—and the pointless, repetitive dialogue strongly resemble the "nonsense plays" of Ring Lardner.[73] This dramatic sketch gave Woollcott a taste for acting and stage writing that led him in both capacities into the theaters several times thereafter.

X   Enchanted Aisles

Of all Woollcott's books, *Shouts and Murmurs* is the only one that is derived wholly from his drama columns, and it is therefore the only one devoted exclusively to his criticism of the drama. Both *Enchanted Aisles* and *Going to Pieces*, though drawn largely from his newspaper and magazine essays about the theater, are really transitional collections that mark the earliest phases of his development from a drama critic to a wide-ranging essayist and eventually to a man of letters.

By the time *Enchanted Aisles* appeared in 1924, Woollcott was

widely recognized as leader of the Algonquin Wits, as drama critic of
the *Herald,* and as a prolific contributor to such popular but influential nationwide publications as *Vanity Fair, Scribner's, The North
American Review, Life,* and *McCall's.* Moreover, since Woollcott
had now mastered the professional writer's trick of multiple exposure, many of the best things in his books had already gone through
several previous versions in other publications. Though his editors
had established a special watch for Aleck's reduplication and
combination of materials—for his tendency, in short, to "plagiarize
himself"—he seemed to know which of his pieces would thrive
under repeated exposures; and the constancy of his reader interest
proved him right.

In *Enchanted Aisles,* a fitting title suggested by Deems Taylor,[74]
Woollcott openly concedes the power of his personal biases and
splits his essays and sketches into two sections—"Enthusiasms" and
"Resentments." Though most of the essays deal with the theater, his
"Enthusiasms" are represented by several magazine pieces that belong more properly among his mature and whimsical essays upon
personalities or character types outside the theater world. Some are
literary portraits like "Mr. Tarkington" and "Stephen Crane."
Others are sketches about artists or scholars like "Neysa McMein,"
"Irving Berlin," and "Copey." Still others are nostalgic war
memories like "Madame Cocaud" and "The Letter of Monsieur
Aimé." There are also " '*Malbrough s'en va-t-en guerre,*' " which is a
historical sketch about the origins of a revived French song, and
"The Paris Taxi-Driver Considered as an Artist," which is one of
Woollcott's most engaging sentimental sketches about a famil-
iar character type. Likewise, the last four of his twelve
"Resentments"—"The Speaker of the Evening," "The Passing of the
Thanatopsis," "Bon Voyage," and "De Senectute"—have nothing to
do with the theater.

But the rest of the pieces in *Enchanted Aisles* are an extension of
Woollcott's long experience as drama critic; and, even more than
Shouts and Murmurs, this collection helped to make the stage anecdote a popular literary form. As one might expect, most of
Woollcott's "Enthusiasms" take the form of biographical essays
about theater people. Some of his characters are highly eccentric,
like de Pachmann and his amazing recitals, in which the pianist
"with many winks, chuckles, groans, and appeals to heaven, keeps
up a continuous murmurous chatter about the music he is invok-

ing." Others are giants of a lesser mold, like Elsie Janis, "The Most Strolling Player," whose sheer versatility as a worldwide barn-stormer, vaudeville star, commedienne, and chanteuse could not keep her from performing in sedate concert halls as well. Still other kinds of essays deal with entire theatrical productions, like those that Woollcott discusses with disarming loquacity and candor in "The Six Best Plays." Here he mulls over all the conflicts and va-garies that influenced the selection of the six plays he enjoyed most, openly admitting that, after "much rumination and anxious preci-sion," he realized that his list did not contain the six plays he had most enjoyed, but the six that he would most like to see again if they were well played. To be totally honest about the plays that he had most enjoyed when he first saw them, Woollcott confessed, he would have to list "The Arabian Nights," a certain animal act, The Royal Lilliputians, and "The Survival of the Fittest." The first three he had seen as a child, and the fourth was so "wildly atrocious" a performance that Woollcott had "never enjoyed a play more."[75]

By far the most intense of Woollcott's "Enthusiasms" are a half-dozen essays upon the most famous contemporary or near contem-porary stars of stage and screen. Nowhere in American dramatic criticism is the tone of sheer idolatry more pervasive than in "Bern-hardt," where Woollcott pays tribute to that almost legendary ac-tress who, in the months before she died at seventy-eight, had retained her incredible energy and had seemed to the impression-able critic "a ruin . . . with a bit of gay bunting fluttering jaunty and defiant from the topmost battlement." But other worshipful essays are titled "Duse" and "Mrs. Fiske," and each is in its own way a minor masterpiece of appreciative criticism. Speaking of Eleanora Duse as the greatest actress of the nineteenth century, Woollcott says that her return to the New York theaters with ten plays in 1923 was "a reunion, a tribute, and a dream come true" for those to whom her acting seemed "as though the loveliest sculpture you had ever seen were come magically to life."

And for Mrs. Fiske, his acknowledged favorite among all living actresses, Woollcott reserves an appreciative essay that is a prodigy of indirection. Having already published his book about Mrs. Fiske's views of the theater, he now returns to her with what was soon to become his mature and tested technique for letting a person spring to life through the apparently random and inconsequential use of anecdote, related references, and multiple viewpoints. Be-

ginning with an account of the offhand way in which St. John Ervine
wrote his uncharacteristically frivolous play *Mary, Mary, Quite
Contrary,* Woollcott follows the manuscript to Belasco's reopening
of his own theater with Mrs. Fiske in the leading role. In just this
pertinent yet sidelong fashion Woollcott gets to his subject, and he
reveals in so doing the essential qualities of Mrs. Fiske's talent by
suggesting the improbability that Ervine had written the role for
"any one so nervous, so darting, so brittle, so gleaming as Minnie
Maddern Fiske," an actress who nonetheless touched the play with
"the most electric hand in the theater."

Unfortunately, similar techniques of reminiscence and anecdotal
association do not work so well in the essay on Pauline Lord, for the
result is strain and overbalance. Sometimes, as in the account of the
various tributes to John Drew on his fiftieth anniversary in the
theater, these same techniques prove adequate but no more.

As might be expected, "Mr. Chaplin" is one of the most fervent of
Woollcott's "Enthusiasms." Though the critic was later to declare
unequivocally that there is "something false and ugly in the very
idea of a talkie,"[76] he was convinced that silent films were the near
perfect medium for the "matchless art" of Charlie Chaplin, who was
"so sensitive, so delicately and exquisitely graduated a player that
one is apt to overlook the warm humanity and the crafty inventive-
ness that are in the episodes which make up his pictures."

Woollcott rounds off his theatrical "Enthusiasms" with "In 1897,"
"Our Betters," and "An Open Letter to a Lady." The first of these is
a plea for Booth Tarkington or George Ade to write a good period
comedy in the "milestones" manner, in which the quaint speech and
fashions of President McKinley's time would come to life. The second is a special tribute to the students at the Professional Children's
School—those "children of the theater" who "were wage earners at
an age when most of us are loafers"—and to their production of
Merton of the Movies, which had so impressed Woollcott that he
invited all his favorite theater friends to see it with him. As the last
of his theatrical enthusiasms in *Enchanted Aisles,* he assumes the
identity of "the American Playgoer," and over this signature he
sends a Christmas message to Maude Adams, "to carry the seasons
greetings and tell a little of how much we miss you."

Altogether, Woollcott's "Enthusiasms" form what is probably the
most impressive collection of essays in "appreciative criticism" since
William Hazlitt had paraded the beauties of Shakespeare in the

early nineteenth century. But, to balance his enthusiasms, Woollcott provides also a dozen "Resentments." These mature essays in dramatic criticism afford the reader a concentrated exposure to Woollcott's special blend of acerbity and wit. Together with the "Enthusiasms," these "Resentments" are an honest reflection of Woollcott's personal preferences in theatrical matters. Though nearly half of his "Enthusiasms" are concerned with particular actors and actresses, not a single performer and only one playwright, Maeterlinck, are among his "Resentments." Most of his resentment is directed at theater advertising, types of plays, and misconceptions about the theater, especially on the part of critics.

In two "Resentments," for instance, he makes great fun for himself and for his readers when he devises imaginary newspaper advertisements. Those for "In 1944" grow from his mock speculations and predictions concerning the probability that "the Theater of To-Morrow" (a phrase utilizing the title of a book by Kenneth Macgowan) would in twelve specific ways "bear a haunting resemblance to the Theater of To-day," and could easily produce such advertisements as: "THE THEATER GUILD, Roland Young (Sole Director) presents 'INDIGESTION,' a drama of alimentary passions by Eugene O'Neill, with Helen Westley as *Gastritis.*" Similarly, he rails in "Unfamiliar Quotations" at the widespread advertising practice of "discreet deletion"—of using only those portions of bad reviews that can be made to seem complimentary. Yet he wonders what would happen if all advertisements were as candid as the deliberately sarcastic one that had really appeared: "The notoriously bad actor GEORGE ARLISS in a new play on that hackneyed theme, Americanism, 'POLDEKIN,' by the well known hack writer, BOOTH TARKINGTON."

Three of the "Resentments" are leveled against the persistence with which several specific kinds of plays appear in the theater. "A Few Annoying Dramas" contains four samples of plays that irk and defeat reviewers because the productions, neither fine nor terrible, afford the reviewer nothing to evaluate. "The Incautious Drama" is a form of dirge for the many potentially good plays that do not make adequate use of suggestion and that fail as the result of a single unnecessarily explicit scene wherein taste is violated or illusion shattered. "The Helpful Drama" begins as a report about the miraculous moral conversions that Channing Pollock's *The Fool* had wrought in people who saw that play about a man who "tried to live like Christ," but the report ends as a spoof upon plays that are wrongly praised for having done "good" in the world.

"The Essence of Acting" is an outburst of resentment against those drama critics who "are forever trying to hide from the fact that acting is essentially an expression of emotion." Such critics, contends Woollcott, are always complaining that actors "always play themselves." They habitually use the term "an emotional actress," apparently under the impression that there is some other kind of actress, though they are probably overreacting against all the stage anecdotes "about players who could wring sobs from a basilisk by repeating the alphabet in a sufficiently touching manner." In a similar tone, Woollcott writes "The Dissenter," in which he rails against the "professional dissenter" among the critics—the kind who make it their business always to be with the minority in any question concerning dramatic excellence and who are always faced with "the tedious necessity of waiting to learn how the yokelry of the majority will vote."

Maurice Maeterlinck, "the sedulous symbolist from hapless Belgium," is, as noted earlier, the only person who earns for himself one of Woollcott's "Resentments," and in "Maeterlinck" Woollcott openly declares that the author of *Pelleas and Melisande* "is, as the quaint phrase goes, the bunk." It was of the "perfumed posturing" in one of Maeterlinck's plays that Tallulah Bankhead had once whispered to Woollcott, "There is *less* in this than meets the eye."

XI   Going to Pieces

By 1928, Woollcott had gone from the *Times* to the *Herald* and to the *World*; and he had become so oppressed by the relentlessly routine demands of the daily reviewing that his reaction increased his desire to enjoy the self-determination of the free lance. Having turned into an avid gourmet, socialite, and globetrotter, he had no wish to abandon the theater that was ever a part of him; but he wanted the freedom to expand his horizons, to encompass everything of the bizarre or the trivial that appealed to his fancy, and to use that which he knew would appeal to the fancy of his readers. Nonetheless, the backlog of his uncollected essays was still heavily theatrical.

As a result, his next collection of previously published works is ostensibly a theatrical volume with a theatrical title, even though more than a third of the book is devoted to essays that roam freely

among such trivial or sensational subjects as are suggested by these
last two section titles: "On Croquet, Murder, Old Magazines and
the Like" and "City-Room Memories." By this time, however,
Woollcott seems to have made a distinction between his work as a
drama critic and his career as a general essayist; he no longer mixes
his pieces indiscriminately, as he did in *Enchanted Aisles* but deliberately separates them and gives each group its own heading. In this
respect, *Going to Pieces* is the last bridge on a long route that leads
to his two best-selling collections of broadly miscellaneous but carefully grouped essays, tales, and sketches, *While Rome Burns* and
Long, Long Ago.

Going to Pieces, with its obvious *double-entendre*, is not only the
title of the book but also the title of the keynote essay, which is
taken from a rather cute but revealing phrase in the essay: "What
follows, then, is the apologia of one who spends his days and nights
in going to pieces." It is Woollcott's confession that his life work has
thus far been "at least as incredible and as highly specialized as the
polishing of cannons or the antiquing of what-nots," and that, like
most people, he had reached his station in life "through the blind
operations of inconsiderate chance." For the benefit of those large
numbers of young people who are "secretly, though vaguely, resolved to become dramatic critics," he details the steps by which he
became a leader in the "Smart-Aleck school of criticism" in a profession where writers form two classes, "those who become dramatic
critics and those who write editorials deploring the low state into
which dramatic criticism has fallen in our time."

A considerable number of the theatrical essays in *Going to Pieces*
are biographical sketches of famous theater personalities, though
most of the pieces are by this time less like reviews or dramatic
criticism than like the mature personal essays of his later collections.
Many of them are documents on stage history that are no less valuable for the charming fashion in which they are told.

By far the longest of these is "A Mother of the Two-a-Day," the
story of the redoubtable Minnie Marx and her sons whom she
squeezed, cajoled, parlayed, and at last catapulted into show business success by the sheer force of her faith, determination, and
ingenuity. Utilizing a galaxy of anecdotes, Woollcott traces the
career of the zany Marx brothers from their childhood theatrical
billings as The Three (and then Four) Nightingales and The Six
Mascots through their brash career in traveling vaudeville and into

their Philadelphia success in *I'll Say She Is* before they became "fixtures in the landscape of the season" on Broadway.

Among these "theatrical personality" essays, the one titled "In the Path of Pauvre Rachel" is a structural tour de force in which Woollcott presents simultaneously the last tours of two great actresses, Eleanora Duse and Elizabeth Felix, the latter the almost immortal mid-nineteenth century French actress known as "Rachel." Beginning with "Eleanora Duse is dead," Woollcott declares that she "was born on tour and on tour she died," but on that final tour she was "following the footsteps of Rachel," who had come from France to "the gaping savages across the Atlantic" and who was thereby "the first player from overseas to challenge America in a foreign tongue," paving the way for the Italian Duse and at last for a theater grown "frankly polyglot."

There are two highly Woollcottian essays upon the deaths of Gregory Kelly, the popular trouper who had taught Ruth Gordon all he knew about the theater, and of James K. Hackett (in "When Birnam Wood Did Come to Dunsinane"), who was able to "play *Macbeth* to his heart's content whether the public wanted him to or not." One sprightly essay concerns the incredible pantomimic talent of Ruth Draper, who had begun by imitating a Jewish tailor at a house party and who had later become "an indisputable institution" that, "like the Philadelphia Orchestra or any other recurrent boon," performed successfully in foreign countries and was always in complete independence since she needed "no stagehands, no orchestra, not even a theatre."

Proportionately, however, *Going to Pieces* contains fewer essays about theatrical personalities and more about matters of taste than appeared in *Enchanted Aisles;* and this shift of proportion probably reflects Woollcott's gradual shift of perspective from that of drama critic to that of general essayist and litterateur. Even in his speculations upon the theater, questions of taste had begun to be more important than the glamour of the stars. In "Odette, Where Is Thy Sting?," Woollcott castigates one kind of theatrical phenomena that made Woollcott "more than a little ill." It seems that, though Odette Myrtil was not very good at either dancing or playing the violin, she had learned how to do both together, and as a result, she appeared repeatedly in Broadway plays, to seduce some "coy coy baritone" by wildly and exhaustingly dancing to her own fiddling. Such an exhibition causes Woollcott to declare that "the horrid and faintly monstrous incongruity of her art does lie in the undebatable ground of taste," as do other theatrical incongruities that he discusses in the essay.

Yet, as he says in "Holding Nature Up to the Mirror," nothing seems more incongruous than the way in which "the vast majority of people do behave even in the crises of their life according to some pattern they have clipped out of a novel or a movie or a play." And if they do so, he wonders about the moral effects of recent plays "of which the whole point is that the deceived consort flies into a complete calm." He finds the answer in Maugham's *The Constant Wife* in which the playwright suggests that we all should "limit our outbreaks and our revenges to expressions of emotions we actually feel rather than of emotions we think (from too much reading and playgoing) that the neighbors *expect* us to feel."

In "The New Sin in the Theatre," "The Unabated Coyness of Bettina," and "The Dramas that Boom in the Spring," Woollcott decries violations of theatrical taste, decorum, and quality. He complains about the tendency of scene designers to use weak plays for their own showpieces, about the elaborate schemes of stars to prolong and multiply curtain calls, and about the annual decline in the quality of off-season plays. Somewhat apart in structure and in viewpoint from most of these essays is "Poor Carlotta," for it is only superficially a critical commentary upon Clare Eames' portrayal of Carlotta in *Juarez and Maximilian*. Basically, it is a special Woollcottian retelling of the famous tale of the real Carlotta and Maximilian.

Immediately preceding the thematic essay "Going to Pieces," which appears at the end of this section, is a selection of Woollcott's late theatrical reviews under the title "Plays: Pleasant and Unpleasant." These six reviews represent what Woollcott regards as a typical sampling of his reviewing since 1924. According to his own account, he chose them because he knew "no better way to suggest how precipitously varied is the life of a reviewer than by catching up and reproducing here a random handful of clippings from my scrapbook." The reviews are from the columns of the *World* and from *Vanity Fair,* and together they do indeed suggest the range of Woollcott's reviewing in his last years as a professional critic. Five of the reviews concern matters of good taste. Others concern long runs of bad plays and lives of theater people.

Though *Going to Pieces* is Woollcott's last appearance ˎas a professional play reviewer, he actually "quit the routine but never the practice."[77] In his switch to the magazine market, he was simply adapting his carefully wrought reviewing techniques to his growing interest in famous crimes, bizarre personalities, nostalgia, whimsy, and the literary criticism that he had already mastered in his constant evaluation of the fictional forms that had been adapted to the theater. Free to try anything, he turned his talents toward playwriting, radio, lecturing, and book reviewing, but he also maintained a staggering production of top quality magazine material. If anything, his public image became as bizarre and as attention commanding as any that he drew in his most bizarre character sketches, whose popularity became almost a cult among American readers.

CHAPTER 5

Hero Worship and Play Crafting

E XCEPT for Woollcott's early biography of Irving Berlin (1925),
he did not actually "write" his books in the conventional sense.
The day-by-day writing he generally produced, the circumstances
under which he habitually wrote, and the nature of his popularity as
a writer made it almost unavoidable that most of his books would
simply accumulate. The best and most felicitous of his pieces rose
from the mass of his newspaper columns or from his magazine offerings and thereby presented themselves as candidates for successive
compilations. Nonetheless, he could not resist from time to time the
temptation to prove himself capable of deliberately crafting a book;
and, when the subject of such a book was to be one of his idols like
Mrs. Fiske, Charles Dickens, or Irving Berlin, he was willing to
forego his usual activities and even isolate himself in the interests of
getting the job done; and, to a lesser extent, the same procedure
was used to write plays. But his talent was not suited to sustained
writing projects of any kind, and though many of his early attempts
to harness his powers for the long pull may have added a cubit to his
height as a literary figure, none of these volumes proved as lucrative
as his highly marketable shorter pieces.

I Mrs. Fiske

It is strange that a series of interviews should be the basis for the
first published book of a writer who steadfastly refused all requests
to grant interviews. Yet Woollcott, who once remarked to Archibald
MacLeish that "the interview is the dullest and most fatuous form of
journalism,"[1] was grateful for the opportunity to serve as recorder of
whatever "views on the stage" might be offered by that great lady of
the American theater Minnie Maddern Fiske. In her mid-fifties at
the time she consented to talk with Woollcott for publication of her
views, she had made herself famous from coast to coast as the female
118

star in plays by such eminent dramatists as Ibsen, Edward Sheldon, and her own actor-playwright husband, Harrison Grey Fiske. Long besieged by publishers soliciting her memoirs, Mrs. Fiske had always refused to write anything of her own. But when she met the young *Times* critic whose victory over syndicated managers and whose honest admiration for her work had struck a responsive chord in her affections, she readily acquiesced to a series of interviews that first appeared in *Century Magazine* and then in a book published by the Century Publishing Company under the title *Mrs. Fiske—Her Views on the Stage Recorded* (1917).

For years Woollcott had been a devotee of Mrs. Fiske, and the interviews added luster to that devotion, as Chapter VIII of *Shouts and Murmurs* would attest. In that chapter, "Presenting 'Fogg's Ferry,'" Woollcott celebrates Mrs. Fiske's first starring role in New York under her maiden name of Minnie Maddern. The play was a "romantic comedy-drama" of such far-fetched incident and such unsubstantial quality as to give no hint that its girlish star would reach a station in the theater world that would cause publishers to seek her out. But she had come by 1917 to "be more completely identified with the loftier literature of the theater than any other player of her time."[2] Because of her whirlwind schedule, Woollcott had to catch her at odd moments of leisure and sometimes in picturesque surroundings.

Despite his adulation for the celebrated actress, Woollcott frequently played the Devil's Advocate during their conversations, discreetly sparking her replies by posing hypothetical exceptions to her arguments; but he also maintained his proper place as an interviewer. All in all, he accomplished instinctively and with seeming ease that dichotomous dual responsibility of the interviewer: to create and to direct the conversation without hindering or distorting the responses of the subject. Indeed, Woollcott clearly showed that Mrs. Fiske's notorious reticence was really a "deep-seated aversion to appearing in any degree oracular" and that her views upon the theater therefore had to be "gathered largely from the memories of unguarded conversations." Moreover, he did more than merely record these "unguarded conversations"; he used them for maximum effect. He sometimes condensed them; he sometimes stopped to put them into historical perspective; but he always vividly set the scene of the interview to make the reader fully aware of the striking "presence" of Mrs. Fiske.[3]

After Mrs. Fiske's tryout performance of Marian De Forest's *Erstwhile Susan*, their first conversation took place over a platter of omelet, "which refection and the repertory idea we proceeded to demolish at some length and with great gusto" (20). In an age of specialization, she declared, repertory theater was an anachronism that overexposed impressionable actors to bad directors, prevented actors from perfecting difficult roles, and made it impossible to build the ideal cast for the perfect performance.

Then, during tea time on the veranda of the Fiskes' summer home in New Jersey, she avidly berated the "flippant scoffers" (43) who refused to believe that, "rightly projected in the theater, Ibsen always has paid and always will" (47) even though his plays have been "misinterpreted and mangled" (50) by those in America who had failed to see "the color, the romance, the *life* there is in them" (48–49). Confessing that she had turned to the "life-sized work" (60) of Ibsen because she had never been capable of playing the love scenes in lesser plays, she described the completeness with which she had re-created the entire life of Hedda Gabler in the "ghost theater" (63) of her mind before she had tried to play the part.

Next, picking up the thread on which the previous interview had ended, she talked about "The Actor in the Making" while she and Woollcott dined in an Italian restaurant on Bleecker Street. Defending her belief that there is, or ought to be, "a complete technic [*sic*] of acting" (76) that would justify a national conservatory of acting, she offered the priceless opinions upon the histrionic art for which publishers had waited so long. The voice, she said, "is the beginning and the end of acting" (82). And despite her dislike for the oracular, she delivered a battery of axioms: "an actor is exactly as big as his imagination" (82); the serious actor must be "reflective" and avoid becoming "theatricalized" (86); he must not "be corrupted by the director," and he must above all "*ignore* the audience" (89); he cannot safely "trust any player's analysis of his own psychology" (99); and "the greater the artist, the less keenly need he feel" (100).

Some time later, when Mrs. Fiske and Woollcott met again over tea and orange marmalade on the veranda of a colonial farmhouse in Connecticut, Mrs. Fiske declared that a truly American national theater would have to be a traveling company that would bring the theater to the people under an "ideal director"—"an amiable and gifted tyrant" (123)—who could teach young people to act and who would particularly train them not to see all plays exclusively in terms of their own roles.

During their last encounter, Woollcott escorted Mrs. Fiske to a matinee, where her perceptive queries and comments upon the performances provided the substance of the chapter. As they waited for the curtain to rise, she asked about the "fairly celebrated actor" who was the star. "Does he know his business?" she inquired of Woollcott. "Has he vitality? . . . dignity? . . . *distinction?*" (146). "Style," she announced, is usually that very set of "mannerisms" for which only the actor, among all the artists, is scolded, and that is why the greatest actors have "always played themselves" (157–60).

These five chapters about Mrs. Fiske conclude Woollcott's attempt "to chronicle her table-talk, faintly, but faithfully" (185). To these chronicles, however, he appends a postscript setting forth his own reactions to Mrs. Fiske's theories; and he includes a qualified demurrer against her rejection of the repertory system and a full chapter upon her life in the theater. After listing all her roles from data gleaned from newspaper files, he closes with his final estimate: that the art of Mrs. Fiske is "acting in its highest estate" (228).

Though Woollcott's first book did not reach vast numbers of readers nor swell his pockets with coin, it enjoyed the respect of a few careful reviewers like the one for the New York *Times*, who said that "no one who is in the least interested in the theatre . . . can fail to find the book fascinating and stimulating."[4] Indeed, as a substantial contribution to theatrical lore and history, *Mrs. Fiske* was selected by a national jury of critics as one of the best books of 1917.[5] Moreover, the interviews had a lasting impact upon Woollcott's attitudes as a drama critic, for many of Mrs. Fiske's notions became Woollcott's critical principles.

II Mr. Dickens Goes to the Play

For Woollcott, the publication of *Mrs. Fiske* was both a tour de force and a *succès d'estime*. Though the Shubert affair had given him early fame, nothing in his first few years as a drama critic had suggested to publishers that he might have a good book in him. Coming so early in his career, this book—a "scoop" in newspaper parlance—served notice on publishers that Woollcott was worthy of serious attention. With *The Command Is Forward*, he justified the implicit promise that he could be expected to get things done in the publishing world; and by the end of 1922, he had published not only *Shouts and Murmurs* but also a combined Dickens commentary and compilation.

Mr. Dickens Goes to the Play is a pioneering book of its kind. According to Woollcott's prefatory account, he became aware of the need for such a volume when the Irish actor J. M. Kerrigan said it was "a cruel pity that all this Dickens talk and streeleen on the theatre is not caught up in one volume." At that time there were, in fact, two books dealing with Dickens' various theatrical involvements,[6] but none that brought together a sampling of the Dickens material in such a way that, as Kerrigan had phrased it, "a man could be finding it of a fine Christmas afternoon." Woollcott's book filled this long-felt gap in Dickens biography, serving as "a double contribution to the bibliography of the novelist and of the stage," [7] and it helped spur a revival of interest that produced two other books on the subject within five years.[8]

Moreover, the Dickens book revealed in Woollcott a surprising capacity for thorough but unpretentious scholarship that, in his abhorrence of formal academics, he veiled behind the chatty and often sprightly tone of his prose. As one reviewer noted, Woollcott's material on Dickens had been "carefully culled and piously arranged."[9] Yet, as with the book on Mrs. Fiske, Woollcott was not content merely to record or to compile the words and ideas of another person, however flagrantly he might idolize his subject. He insisted upon doing whatever seemed necessary to interpret, to highlight, and to enliven his subject.

In the Dickens book, he provides two introductory chapters that are characteristic Woollcottian essays upon the theater. The first is a profusely allusive demonstration of the fact that "the mummers" in Dickens' novels are both more contemporary and more nearly deathless than the other characters—that they are, indeed, "a throng of immortals." He then contends that a complete shelf of Dickens contains "some of the best dramatic criticism in the language" since it "bristles with texts for every writer on the theatre." The second chapter is openly a thesis essay titled "The Thwarted Actor," wherein Woollcott employs every appropriate device of evidence and rhetoric to prove that the most celebrated British novelist of the nineteenth century was really "a natural-born leading man" who might have been "the overtowering actor" of his age "had not chance otherwise canalized his great genius." To prove his thesis, Woollcott summons incidents and anecdotes from every corner of Dickens' life and work: he cites the novelist's youthful attempts at playwriting, his "pantomimic gyrations" while composing, his "comically transparent excuses for appearing in amateur dramatics," and his "adoration of Macready," for whose private approval he wrote most of the great narrative scenes that became his public readings.

In the chapters containing Dickens' personal correspondence about theatrical matters, Woollcott performs a service that was long wanting in Dickens scholarship. Using the original copies of the letters in the Pierpont Morgan collection, he restores the many names and passages that the Dickens executors, in an access of Victorian overnicety, had deleted from the standard "family edition" of the correspondence. Since Woollcott also does everything possible to verify matters that "the often cryptic pages of Forster's biography" had made obscure or misleading, the result is a fully restored selection of the letters that Dickens wrote from 1838 to 1868 to his close friend Macready. These letters were sent from America, France, and several residences in England; and they intimately discuss mutual friends in the theater, Dickens' attempts at playwriting, Macready's performances, Dickens' public readings, the Covent Garden fire, and the American and French theaters in general. There is also an equally revealing selection of "Miscellaneous Letters" upon Dickens' highly varied theatrical concerns from 1837 to 1866 which were sent from many locations in England, Europe, and North America to family, friends, actors, managers, critics, and business associates.

Other sections of the book contain carefully edited passages about the theater from *Sketches by Boz, David Copperfield, Little Dorrit, Great Expectations,* and *The Uncommercial Traveler,* along with the entire section on "The Vincent Crummles Company" from *Nicholas Nickleby.* Woollcott ends with a survey of the various dramatizations that had been made from Dickens novels and with an appended "playbill" of conjuror's tricks devised by Dickens, "who was no mean conjuror" himself.

Although the general tone of Dickens' theatrical correspondence is one of high excitement, involvement, and intensity, one senses that Woollcott's enthusiasm has transcended the evidence relative to his interpretation of Dickens' mastery of the theater. One cannot quite accept the intimation that Dickens' magnificent novels owe their existence largely to the sheer frustration of a man who would far rather have been an actor, a theater manager, or a playwright. The "thesis" of the first two chapters is never quite borne out by the rest of the book; and, though *Mr. Dickens Goes to the Play* is an important document in both Dickens biography and theater history, it does little to alter the generally accepted notion that, at best, Dickens brought to the theater "the infectious spirit of the supreme amateur."[10]

III   The Story of Irving Berlin

Until 1924, Woollcott had never attempted a sustained piece of writing. His longest pieces had been the Sunday essays for the drama pages of newspapers, a variety of occasional articles for the magazines, and the two introductory chapters for the Dickens compilation. Even in his volume on Mrs. Fiske, his own writing had been confined to a short and brilliant burst of scene setting at the opening of a chapter or to the paraphrases and the commentaries that bound together the long transcriptions of Mrs. Fiske's "tabletalk." Everything in his training as a writer, every rhetorical device and trick of organization, had suited him for the high specialty of the short essay, and particularly for the quick "personalized" sprint in prose.

But when he retired to Enos Booth's summer house on Neshobe Island in the summer of 1924, he had prepared himself to write a biography that—though not so long as biographies often go—would require that he sustain a single piece of writing for two or three hundred pages. His choice of subject, the early and as yet unfinished life and career of Irving Berlin, was one that might have been expected of Woollcott. Like Mrs. Fiske and Dickens, as well as the subjects of dozens of Woollcott's articles and essays, Irving Berlin was the kind of special hero of whom Woollcott could say that his life story had "a strong appeal to my foolish and romantic heart."[11]

Yet it is perplexing that for his first book-sized job of writing he would undertake a task so fraught with nearly insurmountable difficulties. Insufficiently versed in the technicalities of composing music, he had to rely almost exclusively upon the testimony of such musical technicians as Jerome Kern and John Alden Carpenter for whatever authority his book could carry in the realm of musical composition. Worse yet, the biography could not be a complete one, since in 1924 Berlin was only thirty-six years old, with every likelihood that his career would be even longer and more spectacular than it had been. There was also the possibility, as Woollcott openly admitted, that by the end of Berlin's life his songs would be forgotten altogether.

All these dangers Woollcott recognizes in the last few pages of his book, along with the concluding observation that no responsible writer could possibly tell the "essential part of the full story" of any man "who, in time and space, lives just around the corner and may himself read the words that you have written." This apologia, however, also makes one wonder why Woollcott attempted a subject for which such an apology had to be made. This problem raised in Louis Kronenberger's mind an almost rhetorical question: "What is the significance of writing about a man if his picture, far from being rounded or complete, is to be deliberately concealed from the reader's eye?"[12]

These were the difficulties that beset Woollcott when, with characteristic energy, he settled down on Neshobe Island to tell the story of the Russian-Jewish immigrant boy Israel (Izzy) Baline, who changed his name to Irving Berlin because that was the way people pronounced his last name, though George M. Cohan was to charge him amicably with being "a Jew boy that had named himself after an English actor and a German city."[13] To offset these problems, Woollcott had stuffed his head full of information gleaned from interviews with friends of Berlin in New York, from letters from composers, and from his own well-stocked memories of the era when Berlin had risen from poverty to prominence in the best Horatio Alger tradition.

The result is a crowded panoramic study of the sometimes half-lit, sometimes garish and brassy world that could spawn an Irving Berlin, a world of which Berlin was an integral part, but one in which the central figure is seen always from the outside. In an attempt to tell the story of Irving Berlin without offending the living subject by speculating upon his conflicting motives and inner struggles, Woollcott falls back upon the story-telling device he had always used supremely well—the anecdote. Indeed, he tries to write biography by means of anecdote; and he should not have been surprised that the result is not really biography but a lively, colorful, fast-paced, entertaining study in the social and cultural history of an era, with Irving Berlin as its central figure. Had he far more accurately used the title *The World of Irving Berlin*, he would have satisfied his critics better.

The opening pages introduce the reader to Izzy Baline as a ragamuffin newsboy who maintains his clutch on five precious pennies even while nearly drowning in the East River. But succeeding chapters quickly become, first, a study of the trials of Russian-Jewish immigrants in the New York ghettos of the 1890s,[14] and second, a sequence of brilliant anecdote clusters that illustrate what life was like for the busker of the Bowery, for the singing waiter in notorious Chinatown saloons and dance halls like Nigger Mike Salter's, for the slightly higher class singing waiter in song-and-dance hangouts like Jimmy Kelly's in Union Square, and for the struggling young lyricist in the composers' sweatshops of Tin Pan Alley and Broadway during the second decade of the twentieth century. At this point, in a short interim between rags and riches, the recurring figure of Irving Berlin becomes the soldier-troubador of World War I who returns home to merge with the world of high-powered song plugging in which one with "a gift of inexhaustible melody" (6) could find the wealth and the fame that the American Dream so lavishly offers even the least of those who do not merely yearn but also labor.

The rest of the story of Irving Berlin is really that of The Music Box, "a small, jewel of a theater that should be the chummy home of a succession of such revues as those revels of girls and music for which America had already become famous to the ends of the earth" (176–77). True, the idea for The Music Box had first germinated in the active mind of Irving Berlin, but, as Woollcott tells the tale, the whole fascinating story of the enterprise was hardly more Berlin's than Sam Harris's or Joseph M. Schenk's or Grace Moore's.

Altogether, Berlin emerges as a kind of current legend; he is a fabulous and unlikely figure whose inexplicable talent serves as the bottomless well-spring of words and melodies so often heard in every corner of the world—ones that are so thoroughly imbued with the quality of folklore that they seem not to have been written by a man at all but to have sprung spontaneously from the lives of the people. During those years after 1911 when Berlin "was to let no season pass without at least one riotous success,"[15] he left a heritage of songs that linger in the collective memory of his own and succeeding generations. In Woollcott's book the reader can momentarily share the world in which they came to life. But relative to Irving Berlin, as Douglas Moore points out, "the reader wonders vainly what he is really like."[16]

One cannot know, for in Woollcott's book Berlin becomes a living legend without having quite come to life as a man. The reason for this peculiar shortcoming is only partly to be explained by Woollcott's declaration that he had consciously done no more than compile "a source book for the wiser historian who will put the facts in permanent form" (223). A deeper reason, one that belies John Farrar's suggestion that Woollcott "could write a great biography,"[17] is that to do so Woollcott would have had to submerge his own personality—and, of all the writers of his day, he was one of the least likely to possess this special capability.

IV   The Channel Road *and* The Dark Tower

After writing his book on Irving Berlin, Woollcott never again attempted a full-sized biography, or, for that matter, any other sustained writing projects except two plays with which he rather fondly hoped to achieve success in those Broadway theaters where he had served for years as a critic. His closest friends—Robert Sherwood, George Kaufman, Marc Connelly, Ring Lardner, Edna Ferber, and several others—were writing successful plays. Yet for wit, style, and critical acumen none of his friends was more widely celebrated than he. Woollcott could not rest in conscience or in professional pride until he had fully measured himself as a playwright.

To Woollcott, it seemed sensible—but as a practical matter it did not prove entirely fortunate—that he should enter the lists with the expert help of Broadway's most successful and most versatile collaborator, George S. Kaufman,[18] with whom, eventually, he wrote and produced both *The Channel Road* (1929) and *The Dark Tower* (1933). In August 1919, Woollcott had returned from the war to find Kaufman behind the drama editor's desk in the *Times* offices. As first string drama critic, Woollcott was still the ranking employee, the senior member of the drama department, who was commonly known among the smaller deer as "God's big brother." But Kaufman was keen-witted, independent, fast-working, uncannily knowledgeable about the theater, and as second string drama critic, monumentally unimpressed by the fearsome reputation of his immediate superior. Moreover, he could match Woollcott idiosyncrasy for idiosyncrasy.

As wits, critics, journalists, literary men, and unique personalities, these men were worthy of each other; and the close association they maintained throughout their lives was characterized as much by incessant intellectual contest as by mutual respect for each other's uniqueness. In a fit of exasperation, Woollcott once remarked that "Mr. Kaufman has always been careful to treat me like dirt."[19]

In a collaboration, this interaction of personalities was unlikely to create the intricate balance necessary to success. As a result, both of the plays that emerged from the Kaufman-Woollcott teamwork suffer from imbalances that suggest that the melding of their talents was impossible. In each play, for instance, Kaufman seems to have devoted most of his attention to the technical aspects of the composition and to have done so without making use of Woollcott's keen sense of dramatic timing. On the other hand, Woollcott seems to have worked mostly with dialogue and characterization; and he committed excesses because he did not call upon Kaufman's spare and pointed sense of verbal economy in stage writing. Moreover, Woollcott could not have been the easiest of collaborators since he had spent a lifetime establishing himself as incontrovertible authority upon certain matters, and it was hardly worth chancing his wrath to suggest that he might need advice in these areas.

In the writing of *The Channel Road*, Kaufman may not have been very enthusiastic about the arrangement from the beginning. Though for several years the two critics and fellow Algonquin Round Tablers had spoken in a purely speculative manner about the possibility that they might one day write a play together, Woollcott's access of enthusiasm for the project had found Kaufman still concerned about the success of *June Moon*, which he had just finished writing and producing with Ring Lardner. Moreover, as Teichmann suggests, the projected script "was not Kaufman's 'cup of tea,' but rather than refuse Woollcott the chance to do a play, he plunged into it."[20]

The job that Woollcott had in mind was a dramatization of de Maupassant's widely read story "Boule de Suife" ("Ball-of-Fat" or "Tallow-Ball"), a biting and cynical tale about a group of self-righteous and self-seeking French people who, for profiteering motives of their own, try to escape the German occupation of 1870 by hiring a common stagecoach to take them from occupied Rouen to the channel city of Le Havre. At the inn, they are detained by a German officer who insists upon claiming the favors of a plump prostitute universally known as "Ball-of-Fat," who, to the group's discomfiture, has been their companion from the beginning of the trip. Convinced that the officer will not release them until the prostitute acquiesces, they prevail upon her with every argument at their command. But to their chagrin and frustration, she refuses with a dignity and integrity foreign to their understanding.

At last, however, she succumbs to their blandishments, and especially to the arguments supplied by a nun in the company, who has liberally cited the testaments to prove that God forgives sinners "when the motive is pure." Worn to submission by these pressures, the prostitute purchases the freedom of these "honorable" people by the otherwise gratuitous bestowing of her favors. Next morning when the group assembles to leave in the coach, however, they all "seemed not to see her or to know her," and all the way to Le Havre she weeps at "the scorn of these honest scoundrels, who had first sacrificed her and then rejected her, like some improper or useless article."

In *The Channel Road,* the German lieutenant emerges as a more complex and subtle character than the German officer of the narrative; and according to most of the reviews, the acting of the part was one of the strongest things in the performance. This officer does not desire the prostitute, but lets the group believe that he does; for he is really awaiting authority from his superior to arrest them as profiteers seeking escape to England. He is amused and disgusted at their behavior; and to go through with the farce, he accepts the prostitute into his bed on Christmas Eve but arrests the group the next morning—and permits only the scorned prostitute and the two nuns to go on their way to Le Havre. As a result of this twist, the play acquires a moral force that is altogether lacking in de Maupassant's narrative. Since Kaufman had never felt himself a "literary" man, the selection of this story was probably left to Woollcott, who must also have been largely responsible for shifting its basic mood from the brutally realistic to the satirically comic and for devising the alterations of incident that made possible that tonal shift.

The reviews of *The Channel Road* were strongly mixed, but two or three of them were not only favorable but enthusiastic enough to be almost raves. One of these which appeared in *Catholic World,*[21] was willing to overlook some of the "unnecessary coarseness of speech" in favor of the "satire on that form of respectability which guards its pocketbook and the outward show of morality with equal zeal and pompousness." Another warm review, done by Joseph Wood Krutch for *The Nation,*[22] applauded the co-authors for having the courage to take "most of the main incidents but none of the spirit" of de Maupassant's famous story, in order to show that the events "constitute a contretemps rather than a calamity and that the occasion is one rather for wit than for indignation or tears."

By and large, however, the other reviews ranged from lukewarm to frigid. Writing in Woollcott's old *Times* column, "The Play,"[23]

Brooks Atkinson complimented the authors upon the character drawing and upon the effective shift from de Maupassant's malice to a moral conclusion, but he contended that the play is "in many respects a library drama with a weakness toward fine writing and sentimental phrase-making." In his Sunday column, "The Open Season" (successor to Woollcott's old "Second Thoughts on First Nights"), he complained more strongly against the mode of composition by indicating that his enjoyment of the play was blunted by "the fulsome literary style in which it is written, or rather overwritten."[24] In this complaint he sounded the note that, for most of the critics, seemed to be the most serious weakness of the play. The faces of the characters, said one critic, "may be the faces of de Maupassant's people; but the voice is the voice of Mr. Woollcott talking brightly to himself."[25] Another critic perceptively hinted at the reason behind the stylistic weakness of this otherwise effective comedy: "Woollcott's style, utterly gay as it may be elsewhere, has come down heavily on this story, blotting out much of its sting under the sort of fine writing that turns to lead in the theatre."[26]

Four seasons later, undeterred by the mixed reviews and frustrated by a feeling that the run of The Channel Road had been stunted by the 1929 market crash, Kaufman and Woollcott wrote and produced another Broadway play, The Dark Tower. Again, the basic idea seems to have been Woollcott's, but this time the play was not an adaptation or a translation. The central situation of the melodrama, however, strongly resembles that of Trilby, whose hold on Woollcott's imagination had increased with the years. The villain, a monstrous version of Svengali, is no longer merely sinister but outright vile and malicious. A criminal recently loosed from prison, he practices his hypnotic powers to control, to use, and to destroy the brilliant young actress who is his wife. A revenge play, its success depends entirely upon a villain so monstrous that his murderer seems a hero and a liberator. It is also a play in which the important element of suspense requires the withholding of the murderer's identity until the last few moments.

Since 1929, Woollcott had been writing his "Shouts and Murmurs" column for The New Yorker, where his lightly told accounts of famous murders had found a strong vogue. The Dark Tower was Woollcott's attempt to contrive a successful play by using the sly tone of his retold murders as a vehicle to reenact the old and reliable Svengali story. Once more, however, Woollcott found that he could not achieve the same effects when he transferred these subtle qualities to other literary forms. In fact, Richard Dana Skinner felt that the play "merely wastes the large talents"[27] of the distinguished cast; Brooks Atkinson, who called it "an amiable and amateurish charade," suggested "that Mr. Woollcott could have related the story more pungently in his bouncing Dickensian prose."[28] *Theatre Arts* introduced the authors as "two leading wits who should never have lent their individual talents to collaboration."[29] Woollcott wisely avoided collaboration hereafter and made the most of his unique talents as essayist, tale-teller, and sketch-artist.

CHAPTER 6

Glittering Trivia and Modern Sensibility

CONVINCED that he had "got to be a dramatic critic too young"[1] and that he had been wasting his mature talents in an out-grown job, Woollcott entered upon the last phase of his remarkable career in 1928. More accurately, this phase was one of many careers, and so prodigious was his creative energy that any of those careers alone might have been enough for a less ambitious man. In overlapping sequences he was an anthologist; a playwright; an actor in Broadway plays, with road companies, and in the movies; a radio personality; an "ad man" for luxury products; a world traveler; a lecturer; an indefatigable correspondent; and a relentless writer for the magazines.

As a contributor to magazines, he was a supremely professional one. Beginning with a number of occasional pieces that he sold to augment his critic's income shortly after the war, he steadily accelerated his production until, by 1928, he was satisfied that his future was to be that of the free lance. Habitually an early riser, he worked regularly throughout the morning hours; and he plundered the recesses of his astounding memory to turn out urbane and polished pieces on almost every conceivable subject. Between 1919 and 1940—at the lowest defensible estimate, based only upon indexed materials—he published nearly five hundred articles and reprints in seventeen leading periodicals, besides his dramatic criticism. Two or three hundred of these articles were his "Shouts and Murmurs" pages in *The New Yorker*, which he began writing in 1929 and continued at forty pages a year for about six years. Nearly sixty of the other pieces appeared in only four magazines—*Colliers, The Reader's Digest, Everybody's Magazine,* and *The Century*—and from thirty to forty of the rest were articles in his regular *McCall's* series, "Dr. Woollcott Prescribes" and "Reading and Writing."

132

From these sources came the contents of his two best-selling books, *While Rome Burns*—which went through fifteen large printings between March 1934, and February 1935, and which thereby "conferred upon its author a patent of the higher literacy"[2]—and *Long, Long Ago*, which was published posthumously in 1943. Both of these collections are in the truest sense volumes of literary potpourri; they contain articles, essays, anecdotes, sketches, profiles, retold tales, murder stories, criticism, encomiums, legends, reminiscences, meditations, and reveries from all his published writings and from a few of his broadcasts. Most of the pieces, however, were originally written for the "Shouts and Murmurs" page of *The New Yorker*.

I   *"Shouts and Murmurs"*

In American literature, the "Shouts and Murmurs" page is unique. E. B. White, who was on *The New Yorker* staff from the beginning of Woollcott's association with the magazine, clearly remembers the ambivalent relationship that prevailed between Woollcott and editor Harold Ross:

Woollcott had mannerisms in writing—he liked to talk about "these old eyes" and he liked words like "reticule" and "tippet"—words that made Ross retch. When Ross decided to run a regular column ("Shouts and Murmurs") by Woollcott, Ross made it clear he would have nothing to do with editing it—turned the whole business over to Katharine White, who, with an occasional assist from [Wolcott] Gibbs, managed to keep the peace and get the column into the magazine. It was, incidentally, the only column the New Yorker ever ran that was "justified"—that is, made to come out to a certain length, in this case exactly one page of type. This meant cutting or adding. Only time it ever happened, but Woollcott insisted on it and had his way.[3]

For the first few years, Woollcott tried to "justify" the page with a carefully composed thousand word piece of exactly the right length and written as often as possible around a single theme. But by the mid-1930s, his life was so crowded with playwriting, acting, lecturing, and broadcasting that his *New Yorker* page became more and more often a compilation of jokes, anecdotes, and human interest material that frequently required cutting or other editing—whereupon he would promptly resign. Ross, who "resented his friend's easy command of narrative,"[4] would then reluctantly woo him back. This charade continued for five or six years, during which the "Shouts and Murmurs" page, with all its unpredictable waywardness, remained one of the most widely read features of the magazine.

II   *Radio Personality*

Though stricken with "mike fright" upon his first attempt at broadcasting for the Mutual Network in 1929, Woollcott brought to the art of the radio broadcast the same demand for tone and style that he had required of his written work. Overcoming both his "mike fright" and his initial dislike for the "intrusiveness" of the new medium, he became one of the first real students of broadcasting as a major branch of the communicative arts, and he used the medium as a fresh resource for exploiting all his materials, which had become too repetitive in their written forms. He made himself so much a master of this new medium that he became the first of the internationally known radio personalities. Moreover, he found exquisite personal satisfaction in his new role, since there seems to have been "something about projecting himself into several million parlors at the same time which answered the special requirements of his spirit."[5]

As "The Early Bookworm," he chatted familiarly about the books he liked, infecting his hearers with his own enthusiasms, much as he was doing at the same time in the pages of *McCall's* and frequently in "Shouts and Murmurs." In these "book talks," he seemed less interested in exposing bad books than in convincing people to read good books that had remained undiscovered. As the appreciative critic, he sometimes singlehandedly lifted a book or an author from obscurity into fame, as he did with Yeats-Brown's *The Lives of a Bengal Lancer* or with the whole career of James Hilton.

Ringing his bell regularly as "The Town Crier" over the Columbia Broadcasting System, Woollcott again used and reused all the best of his old material. Yet he adapted the old stories so well for oral presentation that his hearers were as charmed as if the tales had never been heard before. As a result of Woollcott's influence, they listened to the Hamilton Choir and responded to his appeals for the Seeing Eye and other charities as though he were a close friend. Out of this intimate rapport grew the nationwide "Woollcott cult." As James Thurber once remarked, "there was never anything quite like it."[6]

Making the best use of a voice that he had trained to evoke all the responses familiar to his readers,[7] Woollcott "became a stylist, perhaps the first stylist of the art of radio locution."[8] As a result, even though his broadcasts "were generally compounded of emotion and what he called 'incurable triviality,' "[9] he kept all the effects that had been so successful on the printed page. "In spite of its many attempts," writes John Mason Brown, "the radio has produced no one who could touch Woollcott; no one who had his sense of melodrama and suspense; no one who could bite the language with his precision; no one who could tell a story with his skill."[10]

III *Incurable Trivia*

In one sense, everything Woollcott wrote was a form of trivia. Early in his career he had realized that his strength as a writer lay in his extraordinary command of the minor forms of literature rather than in what lies at the top of the "hierarchy of the genres," and he was not apologizing or rationalizing but accepting the proven limits of his talents when he characterized himself as a great writer with nothing to say. He was well aware, however, that a keen eye for trivia had been the special gift of all the best-loved familiar essayists, and he worked with satisfaction in the literary tradition that had allowed Addison and Steele to write about the blooming of tulips in a park or a casual visit to the playhouse; that had permitted Lamb to write quaintly about old china or to indulge in a reverie upon dream children; that had enabled Dickens to take a reader along with him on a night walk; and that had inspired Washington Irving to weave a suspenseful sketch upon the identity of a half-seen fellow lodger or to ruminate upon the ravages of time. Woollcott truly loved trivia, and his trivial pieces at their best possess a rare quality of illumination.

To Woollcott, the delight of trivia was that subjects were numberless and that their appeal was limitless. But, since he could not repeatedly fill large spaces with pure trivia, no matter how pleasingly he wove the material, he found the thousand word space of the "Shouts and Murmurs" page the ideal medium for his infinitely various observations upon the small highlights of human life. There he might chat about anagrams and chide Frank Sullivan for addressing him as "Anagrampa," or he might muse upon pirated volumes of Barrie and other bookish tidbits, upon the early American self-appointed "aristocracy," upon the hoarding of old theater programs, or upon linguistic quibbles, card playing, curious names, versions of ubiquitous tales, croquet—or he might simply pull together an array of jokes and anecdotes that were so loosely connected as to make his *New Yorker* editors speculate that radio broadcasting had ruined him.

Most of the best of Woollcott's trivia was gathered into his books, beginning with *Going to Pieces,* which contained three or four such pieces in a section titled "On Croquet, Murder, Old Magazines, and the Like." Here, he defended his enthusiasms for the "higher and dirtier croquet" ("No Peace Unto the Wicket") and mused upon the distinguished alumni of Hamilton College ("But Why Elihu Root?"). He told enthralling anecdotes to justify the optimism of those fortunate people to whom the "privilege of waking up" each morning seems always a prelude to "the Great Adventure" ("Matins"), and he indulged in mock remorse that he could not write good travel articles because he always enjoyed most the places that are "unmarked in any guidebook" ("As Easy as Rolling off a Travelogue").

In *Enchanted Aisles,* too, he included some pieces upon subjects entertaining in themselves but of limited significance. In "The Paris Taxi-Driver Considered as an Artist," for example, he speculates that the world famous "imaginative driving" of the Paris cabbie had merely perpetuated the adventuresome tradition of the old *cocher* of the carriage days. In "The Speaker of the Evening," he wonders why anyone, including himself, can ever be egotist enough to believe that people at a dinner really want to hear him speak; in "Bon Voyage," he castigates the tradition of the useless bon voyage gift. In "De Senectute," he provides as his own fitting epitaph a list of the trite and outworn expressions he had never been guilty of using in his writing.

Among the fifty-two widely assorted pieces in *While Rome Burns,* seven are sheer trivia, of which "The Editor's Easy Chair" and "This Thing Called They" can be classed as the most interesting sketches in the collection. The former tells of a magnificent chair delivered by mistake to Woollcott's home at Wit's End and retrieved at last by a distraught furniture dealer. The latter sketch is an expanded anecdote in which the vaudeville comedian Jimmy Duffy wreaks supreme vengeance upon an unresponsive audience. Other trivia in this volume appears under "Book Markers" and may be classed as literary sidelights rather than conventional reviews or standard critical commentary. In "The Nostrils of G. B. S.," Woollcott contends that Shaw was not so much an artist as a teacher whose strongest angers were roused by the smell of burning flesh. "Wisteria" is an unfavorable commentary upon the tone of snobbery in the writings of Owen Wister, especially in Wister's memoir of Theodore Roosevelt; and "The Triumph of Newtie-Cootie" is Woollcott's fulsome praise for a book that sets the record straight about President Wilson's maligned secretary of war, Newton Baker.

The largest portion of Woollcott's trivia appears in *Long, Long Ago*, and, being a wider selection, it is more typical of his range since he tended as time went by to make more and more use of trivia. He includes anecdotes or sketches about precognition ("Life Was Worth Living") and about the utter illumination sometimes gained through quick glimpses or chance phrases ("The Face in the Crowd"). He comments upon the appearance of William Gillette, the actor who had created the role of Sherlock Holmes, at a meeting of Holmes worshipers ("The Baker Street Irregulars"). He weaves sketches about small town editors of weekly newspapers ("The Sage of Fountain Inn"), about ingenious ways in which quick-thinking magicians have covered up slips in their routines ("The Breaks"), and about the final letter of Franz Schubert to a friend ("The Last Thing Schubert Wrote"). In his most familiar vein, Woollcott also muses upon the Jane Austen cult ("Jane Austen"), upon A. E. Housman's definition of poetry ("Housman"), upon the choice of a quotation from Shaw as a fitting wedding gift ("Gift Suggestion"), and upon the selection of Edmund Gosse's *Father and Son* as the recent nonfiction book most likely to be read in the year 2100.

A few of these items are more substantial than would normally warrant their being categorized as trivia; in fact, they may be so classified only because they do not clearly fit any other category. Such, for instance, is the story of the first meeting between newly retired Supreme Court Justice Oliver Wendell Holmes, Jr., and newly elected President Franklin D. Roosevelt ("The Judge's Last Opinion"). Such, too, are Woollcott's account of his attempt to do graduate work at Columbia University ("I Might Just as Well Have Played Hooky") and his praise of H. G. Wells' prediction that mankind may yet mature enough to create a Utopian "parliament of man" that would insure the survival of the human species ("Experiment in Autobiography").

In each of these finely spun pieces of literary trivia, the Woollcott touch is unmistakable. Here, as in no other area of his writing, he demonstrates his extraordinary versatility in the sheer variety with which he presents his material. No sketch or essay is quite like any other. His endless anecdotes and relevant digressions afford limitless combinations and permutations in style and structure. At his best, Woollcott is unique in his capacity to mold a trivial idea into an entertaining as well as a valuable piece of literature.

IV   *Tears in These Old Eyes*

Of all the inconsistencies in Woollcott's character, none is more revealing than the strain of unabashed sentimentalism in a man whose public image has been a combination of the "ultimate sophisticate" and the "fabulous monster." Though in any other writer these qualities might appear to be irreconcilable contradictions, in Woollcott they were thoroughly acceptable to a reading public that had gradually become accustomed to regarding him as "a congress of opposing parties."[11] As a result, in the era of the "wise crack," in an era that was spawning literary Realism and dramatic Expressionism, the fearsome Fat Fate of Broadway was successful as a one man school of sensibility, as a herald of the feeling heart.

Sometimes his fondness for children found expression in an essay or a sketch that revealed that he was always a devout "Peter pantheist." His Sunday drama pages had repeatedly eulogized the performances of the Professional Children's School, and in his *New Yorker* page these precocious professionals continued to appear (as in "Moliere, Pocket Edition," April 19, 1930). Other essays found their way into *While Rome Burns*, where "Hansom Is" and "The Little Fox Terrier" capture the amused camaraderie with which Woollcott escorted his goddaughter and other children to plays and circuses.

His fondness for children was rivaled only by his fondness for dogs, and he wrote about them with the curious mingling of affection and respect by which the close fraternity of such devotees recognize each other. In his own dogs, he perceived a disturbing likeness to human beings, and he found particular amusement and satisfaction in writing of them as though they were canny but wayward persons with boundless spirit and ingenuity. Most of them emerge as canine counterparts of the "lovable rascal" that has long been a staple of certain kinds of fiction.

No other dog story in American literature has been more widely read than "Verdun Belle"; and as a result, large numbers of American readers have thought of Woollcott as primarily the author of dog stories like "The Passing of Nicholas" and "My Friend Egon," both of which were collected with "Verdun Belle" and widely read under the title of *Two Gentlemen and a Lady*. Woollcott strengthened that impression in June 1939, when he devoted one of his best-loved broadcasts to "an account of several dogs who, in their wisdom and charity, have befriended the author." He called this piece "Cocaud," the name of a French poodle puppy who was a newcomer to the Woollcott household. As a member of "the brotherhood of the poodle," Woollcott wrote the broadcast and included the script in *Long, Long Ago*.

But Woollcott reserved his most passionate strain of sentiment for the profiles and biographical sketches that he wrote about the people he knew and loved best. Though friendship with Woollcott was always precarious, it was nonetheless a patent of the most intense and dedicated intimacy. The well-known charge that he was not interested in making the acquaintance of any person whose life would not make an interesting profile is at best a half-truth. The fact is that he found dullards intolerable and that he therefore surrounded himself with bright and stimulating people.

When he wanted to get highly personal information from such people, he asked for it unapologetically and with disarming directness, as he did when he wrote to John Gielgud: "I keep in the back of my head a considerable reference library on people like yourself on which I draw at incalculable and disconcerting moments for broadcasts or what I suppose must be called essays."[12] He was, indeed, a serious student of the special literary form known variously as the "profile," the "biographical sketch," and the "short biography"—all latter-day descendants of the ancient form called the "character." His interest in the form is attested by the impressive holdings of "assorted profiles"[13] that were found in his library after his death. His own biographical sketches are distinguished for their rare intimacy of tone and detail, for the sureness with which they depict unusual character traits, and for their emotional involvement.

Besides the special *New Yorker* profiles that he wrote about such people as Kaufman, Connelly, and Harpo Marx,[14] Woollcott wrote dozens of similar ones for other magazines. The general tone of these pieces is a combination of admiration, affection, and nostalgia that appears at its best in his brief sketch about the life and career of

Stephen Foster, "Dear Friends and Gentle Hearts."[15] The others of the kind that Woollcott valued most highly had already appeared in *While Rome Burns*, and they were "My Friend Harpo," "A Portrait of Kathleen Norris," "Our Mrs. Parker," "The Young Monk of Siberia" (Charles MacArthur), "The Good Life" (Laura E. Richards), and the unforgettable essay about Paul Robeson, "Colossal Bronze," which Sharon Brown included in the widely used college anthology, *Present Tense*.[16]

Nothing aroused Woollcott's sensibilities and his penchant for nostalgia more keenly than the death of a dear friend or of a unique figure in the world of arts and letters. To him, either event was a deeply personal loss and a grievous deprivation to the American people. Accordingly, he wrote several "memorial essays" that serve both as tributes and as heightened expressions of this sense of loss. Among the earliest of these is "Stephen Crane," a tribute and a memorial that had been triggered by the appearance of Thomas Beer's biography of Crane. Woollcott placed it among the "Enthusiasms" in *Enchanted Aisles*, and afterward, finding the short memorial essay congenial to the active charge of sentiment in his being, he wrote a series for the *Atlantic*, each of which was called "In Memoriam."[17] The people so memorialized were Annie Sullivan Macy (the teacher of Helen Keller) and Rose Field (both essays reprinted in *Reader's Digest* and included in *Long, Long Ago*), as well as Cornelia Lunt (an eccentric, aged socialite) and Ira Dutton. The latter is ostensibly a memorial tribute to a man better known as the Brother Joseph who for forty years took Father Damien's place among the lepers on Molokai, but it is equally a sentimental essay about the universal nostalgia that afflicts Vermonters who are uprooted from their native state.[18]

In his prose, Woollcott shared his friendships with his readers, and, as Edward Weeks observed upon the appearance of *Long, Long Ago* after Woollcott's death, "In the attic of his mind were hundreds of little boxes . . . and these boxes held the souvenirs of his friends past and present."[19] In the word "souvenirs" lies the key to the mood of nostalgia that prevails in much of Woollcott's writing. The nostalgia lurked just below the surface of everything that he wrote, prompting one reviewer to say, "He has an eye for spring and summer beauty, but the faces he loves most are autumnal."[20] The nostalgic pieces began appearing in the collected editions as early as *Enchanted Aisles*, where one finds a sentimental essay about the little *patisserie* at Savenay, to which Woollcott had become sentimentally attached during the war ("Madame Cocaud"), an essay about the nostalgic flavor of Tarkington's books ("Booth Tarkington"), and a wistful reverie about the dissolution of the old Algonquin poker club ("The Passing of the Thanatopsis").

By far the largest amount of pure nostalgia, however, appears in *While Rome Burns*, which contains at least seven such essays. These are "The Sacred Grove," an account of Woollcott's search for a Böcklin painting; "A Plot for Mr. Dreiser," the story of a crazed, deluded, pathetic girl who had once been a lovely model; "For Alpha Delta Phi," a reminiscence of his days as a fraternity man at Hamilton; "Aunt Mary's Doctor," a reverie about the days when young Georges Clemenceau was a family physician in America; "Charlie—As Ever Was," the warmest of Woollcott's tributes to the art of Charlie Chaplin; "Lest We Forget," a tribute to *Journey's End*, a play that R. C. Sherriff wrote from "his own memories of the war"; and "The Corporal of St. Aignan," Woollcott's memory of a soldier who had been content to spend the war in "the sink-hole of the A. E. F."

Despite the strong nostalgic flavor of *Long, Long Ago*, only a few pieces are basically nostalgic in substance, but they are among the most effective things of their kind. "A Christmas Story," for instance, was one of Woollcott's broadcasts, in which he told the O. Henry-ish tale of a meager Christmas Eve supper smuggled into the Algonquin by two aspiring young troupers; and "Quite a Proposition" is the unlikely story of how Marc Connelly came to write *The Green Pastures*. For the sheer nostalgic tug at the heart string, however, none of these surpasses "Hoofbeats on a Bridge," Woollcott's own reliving of the many times when, as a schoolboy, he had returned home to the Phalanx, and had counted the diminishing distance to the front door by the times the horses' hooves clattered on the bridges.

If Woollcott's trivia sometimes seems too trivial and his sentiment too sentimental, the wonder is that the vast number of his devotees never seemed to worry about his excesses. During that sometimes sophisticated, sometimes despairing, largely materialistic era between the wars, when sentiment could be so easily misunderstood or distrusted, even the most cynical reader sensed that the "honest moisture" on Woollcott's "old lashes" was the unabashed expression of real emotion in one who was not afraid to admit that he was a man of feeling as well as wit. When John Mason Brown declared that Woollcott's "heart is one of the country's largest public gardens,"[21] he also spoke for a nation of readers who were prepared to find in that garden from time to time a splash of too-bright color or an unmodified strain of "Ah-shall-we-ever-forget-the-glamor-of-those days."[22] They knew the garden to be of hues that could be riotous as well as soft, and that the music from the hidden alcove was often sad. It was their garden, and they liked it the way it was.

CHAPTER 7

Popular Legendry and the Appeal of the Horrible

I N the sense that legends are folkloric tales with true but unveri-
fiable origins, Woollcott spent much of his creative energy in
weaving about people and events a special aura of distance, twilight,
and deathlessness that gave his tales the universal appeal of legends.
"All of his pieces have a fairy-tale quality about them," said John
Mason Brown. "He loved to have the past and the present meet, to
give them a double exposure, to see them through bifocal lenses.
Places were for him always peopled by the shades of those who had
been there and by the bodies of those present."[1] It made little
difference to Woollcott, therefore, whether an event was contemporary or whether it was of ancient and untraceable origin. To him, all
tales were as old as the human race.

I The Stream of Legend

This tendency to dress almost everything in the vestments of
legend accounts for his insistence that *Woollcott's Second Reader*
must contain not only stories by Hemingway and Dorothy Parker
but also the preface to an ancient Chinese adventure story that,
"like the *Iliad* or the legends of Robin Hood, . . . is assumed to
have been a slow growth of multiple and unidentified authorship."[2]
This impulse also explains Woollcott's habit of thrusting into
"Shouts and Murmurs" oddments of "legends" that occupy equal
space with current gossip and topical anecdotes. The entire page
titled "Stream of Legend,"[3] for instance, provides examples of the
range and types of "legends" that frequently caught his attention.
There are recurrent legends like the "appointment in Samarra"
tale—"anonymous, unclassifiable, . . . even now adrift on the
great stream of legend, of which the source can never be explored

and into which small, unmapped tributaries pour silently, year in and year out." Upon this stream, explains Woollcott, floats many an "unmistakably legendary" tale to which Woollcott makes his own claim under his "riparian rights" as an author. Moreover, he insists that many a current joke or anecdote is really "a mere fragment, broken off from an older story," which, like so many of the "hospital tales," are really only "part of the great lore of paper-work."

Since Woollcott conceived of anything legendary as a continuum from the indefinite past into the indefinite future, the present seemed to him a kind of fulcrum upon which teetered both of the temporal extremes. Therefore he not only swept fascinating legends out of the past but also invested contemporary tales with the qualities of legend. In *While Rome Burns* he recounts the high coincidence of a "Reunion in Paris": an American authoress browsing in a Paris bookstall finds a children's book that she herself had owned during her childhood in America. Far more widely acclaimed is "Entrance Fee," the legend of the young cadet of Saint Cyr who won a five thousand franc sweepstakes that enabled him to spend one night with France's most celebrated courtesan, Cosette. She compliments the lad by returning to him his own five franc contribution to the cadets' sweepstakes.[4] Woollcott was equally capable of making current "legends" out of contemporary figures whose stature as human beings was either already legendary or capable of being made to seem so. Such, for instance, is "Get Down, You Fool!," an unrecorded "colloquy" between Abraham Lincoln and Oliver Wendell Holmes, Jr.

II   *The Living Legend*

Out of Woollcott's preoccupation with the essential material of "short biography" grew one of his most interesting contributions to American literary forms—the "living legend." No other American writer has so prolifically or so convincingly written of contemporary or near contemporary figures in such a fashion as to make them appear "legends in their own time." Since Woollcott was an inveterate and whole-hearted hero worshiper, his natural bent was to invest the subjects of his short biographies with a combination of folk-heroism and density of memorableness that virtually created large numbers of "living legends."

Aside from those living legends that were more properly a part of his dramatic criticism, this peculiar variety of biographical sketch first began appearing in *Enchanted Aisles* with such essays as those on "Irving Berlin" and on "Copey," the beloved Charles Townsend Copeland of Harvard, the model for Fleetwood in Flandrau's *Diary of a Freshman.*

There are many "living legends" in *While Rome Burns.* "The Truth About Jessica Dermott" is an attempt to "winnow out some of the chaff in the legend" that Pierpont Morgan had built the Maxine Elliot theater as a tribute to his infatuation with the actress whose name he gave to the theater. "The First Mrs. Tanqueray" consists of a climactic arrangement of horrendous anecdotes about Mrs. Patrick Campbell, and "The Mysteries of Rudolfo" raises and leaves unanswered the question asked by all who had known the fashionable impresario Rudolph Komer: "What does he do for a living?" "The Legend of Sleepless Hollow" is a short biography of the vaudeville comedian Joe Cook and his New Jersey home, with its "demented golf course," among other legendary garnishings; and "The Prodigal Father" is a tribute to Frank Lloyd Wright as the "Father of Modern Architecture."

Having discovered that these were among the best-liked pieces in *While Rome Burns,* Woollcott included an equal number of similar tales in *Long, Long Ago.* These are "Required Reading for Meatless Days," a report upon Woollcott's last meeting with George Bernard Shaw, who, at eighty-five, seemed to have become the "Teacher in a measureless classroom"; "The Story of a Refugee," another variation upon the story of Irving Berlin; "George the Ingenuous," a character sketch that established the "George Gershwin legend"; "The House That Jack Built," the story of Jack Humphrey, the founder of the Seeing Eye and also the trainer for the famous Seeing Eye dogs for the blind; and "What the Doctor Ordered," an account of the peculiar fashion in which Clarence Day's *Life with Father* had made of the elder Day a personage who "seems likely to become as familiar a legendary figure as Mr. Dooley or Uncle Remus or Huckleberry Finn."

III *Legends of the Unexplainable*

Whetted by the public appetite for anything that bordered upon the mysterious, Woollcott's sense of the dramatic turned more and more frequently toward legendary accounts of unexplained or unexplainable occurrences, especially when those events involved the awesome, the eerie, the spectral, or the macabre. Sometimes his fascination with these tales drew him into antiquity—as when, in a pervasively awestruck tone, he traced the history of the Great Chalice of Antioch to the time when it appeared among the Century of Progress exhibits ("Believe It or Not").[5] From his travels in Europe, he would relay to his readers an exotic legend about a swindler and the mysterious disappearance of some fabulous emerald jewelry ("The Maharajah's Ear-Rings").[6] At other times, he would doggedly trace down and relate recurrent legends concerning eerie goings on in old houses. In "At 59 Washington Square,"[7] for example, the contemporary residents were without exception haunted by "a feeling of horror, inexplicable, incommunicable" in a house that, as it turned out, had been the morgue for a Potter's Field at some time in the dimness of the past.

In his restless search for these eerie legends, Woollcott did not hesitate to write articles about legends he could not solve or verify. He was likely to use the account of some unprovable mystery as a public appeal for helping him to clear up the unknown, as he did with the tale of "The Hidden House,"[8] an expansive country home that had been camouflaged as a cemetery to keep General Sherman's troops from ravaging it during the Civil War. Apparently Woollcott never discovered the location of that house, even though it presumably still existed at the time he began his search.

This kind of tale found its way into *While Rome Burns* under a special grouping of five stories labeled "Legends," of which all but the classic "Entrance Fee" is a tale of the macabre. These include a sample of the comic macabre in the tale of the young Monte Carlo gambler who dashed his shirt front with catsup and pretended to shoot himself in order to return to the tables and recoup his losses with the bankroll that casino authorities secretly slipped into the pockets of suicides to take the onus away from the casinos ("Rien ne Va Plus"): "One always tells tales of self-slaughter at Monte Carlo," remarks Woollcott at the end of the tale; "It is part of the legend of the principality."

But the other accounts in this group are legends of the true macabre. In "The Vanishing Lady," Woollcott relates a much-circulated, many-versioned tale about an English widow who had unwittingly brought into Paris an isolated case of the black plague and who had died of it there. When her corpse was officially obliterated to prevent panic, this act forced her daughter to search in vain for a mother who, by a general conspiracy of silence, had never existed at all. The eeriness of this tale is surpassed only by that of

"Moonlight Sonata," a gruesome account of a shadowy figure who is sitting in darkness and is plucking gray hairs from the head of a woman he had just decapitated.

Just as eerie is "Full Fathom Five," a legend of the spectral macabre. In this tale the actual appearance of a drowned man's ghost is seemingly proved by the presence of a piece of seaweed identified by a marine biologist as a rare variety that grows only on corpses. For sheer grotesqueness, however, none of these legends can equal "In That State of Life," which is the "lingering legend" of the Marquis of Villolobar, the celebrated Spanish ambassador at Brussels—the courtly, intelligent, accomplished favorite of kings and queens the world over. Behind the ingenious prostheses and cosmetics known only to him, he was actually the legendary "Villolobar monster," born indescribably misshapen. He was permanently bald, had stumps for legs, and possessed only a claw instead of a hand.

IV *Murder as a Fine Art*

In Woollcott's repertoire, the legend of the macabre was a close congener of the true murder tale, a relative of the "unsolved murder mystery, from Lizzie Borden down"[9]; for Woollcott was especially interested in cases that had the most bizarre twists and the brightest splashes of gore. Speaking for those readers whose sensibilities might be offended by Woollcott's special treatment of the "classic" murder tale, one reviewer of *While Rome Burns* identified these accounts as "studies in the vulgar macabre."[10] But the overwhelming popularity of these accounts suggests that such reviews spoke for only a minority of American readers. In fact, John Mason Brown voiced the opinion of the rest when he observed that Woollcott had "so staked his claim on murder as a fine art that one is tempted to feel that De Quincey must have left it to him as a special bequest in his will."[11]

When Woollcott made his own mark upon the form of the classic murder tale,[12] he was only adding a special dimension to a literary phenomenon already well established by Edmund Pearson's *Studies in Murder* and William Bolitho's *Murder for Profit*. Woollcott never tired of acknowledging his indebtedness to these two books; and when a representative of the Library of Congress charged him with the honorary responsibility of recommending a special "crime shelf" for use by President Franklin D. Roosevelt, both books had a prominent place on the "Fact" list.[13]

By holding to the paradoxical assumption that murder is a fact of life and by using the tone of the macabre legend, Woollcott achieved enough esthetic distance to remove his readers from the actuality of a gory murder, even while maximizing the goriness. "People thrill to ghosts, mysteries, crimes," observes Samuel Hopkins Adams; "Woollcott can wallow in blood until the sanguine hue tinges his ink."[14] Yet in retailoring the classic murder yarns, Woollcott rarely overpaints the material itself, as he sometimes does in his sentimental tales. Though he sometimes overpsychologizes in an attempt to make a murderess like Lizzie Borden seem more interesting as a person than she might really have been, his depiction of the crime itself—however steeped in carnage or perversion—is usually consistent with the known facts. Indeed, the flippant tone in which he sometimes relates these tales is particularly effective as underplaying rather than as an example of the "laying it on" technique of murder narrative.

In Woollcott's books, the first evidence of his preoccupation with the retold murder story is the appearance of "The Theory and Lizzie Borden" in *Going to Pieces*. Pearson's treatment of the tale in *Studies in Murder* had apparently triggered something in Woollcott's mind, and he had become such a determined digger into the intimate details of murder lore that his version of the Borden multiple murder was only the first of several dozen distinctively Woollcottian retellings of classic crimes. But the grisly tale of Lizzie Borden, "the most absorbing murder case in the annals of America," remained his favorite.[15]

As a serious student of the literature of murder, Woollcott repeatedly turned to the *Notable British Trials* series as both a source and a model. The crime collection of his own library contained twenty-five or thirty of these volumes, along with sufficient other studies that, "if one book didn't cover the subject down to the last microscopic bits of flesh under the fingernails, it was supplemented."[16] Indeed, Woollcott, who borrowed from these volumes quite shamelessly, theorized publicly that the last vestige of the ancient tradition of the retold "fireside tale" was the modern retold murder story, whose "strange craftsmen seek not so much to chronicle a case unknown to their colleagues . . . as to pick up one of these old wives' tales and retell it a little better than it has been told before."[17]

Regarding himself as a kind of champion among these "strange craftsmen," Woollcott openly plundered the *Notable British Trials* for such accounts as that of Madeleine Smith, who put into her sweetheart's cocoa "enough arsenic to have disposed of twenty lovers,"[18] but was released on a verdict of "Not Proven." He complained bitterly that the series did not contain the trial of Christiana Edmunds, who had tried to kill her lover's wife with poisoned bonbons, but who had killed a neighbor boy instead;[19] and he was happy that an "American Trials" series had begun, even though it had managed to make some sensational cases appear dull.[20] When he could not get the necessary information from the British or American trials series, he turned to Smith's *Famous Trials of History* for the story of Ethel Le Neve, mistress of the notorious Doctor Crippen, who had hanged for the murder of his wife. At other times he consulted Duke's *Six Trials* or Walbrook's *Murders and Murder Trials*, or he searched newspaper accounts and hounded people for obscure facts. With this material he enlivened his tales, frequently using it to fabricate comprehensive essays upon various aspects of murder lore, as in "Murder for Publicity,"[21] where he discusses Jack the Ripper, Dr. Cream, and the Hall-Mills case as classic examples of highly publicized murders. Sometimes he even ransacked the writings of his own contemporaries, as in "The Thanatopsis Murder Case,"[22] a broad parody of S. S. Van Dine's novels that uses several contrived footnotes, has a hero named Philo Nance, and bears the signature of S. S. Van Woollcott.

For sheer gore, no murder seems to have had greater fascination for Woollcott than the shooting of Herman Rosenthal, whose riddled body he saw in June 1910 as it lay on the sidewalk outside the Hotel Metropole. In an article devoted to the appearance of bodies in trunk murders, he confessed, "Of all the *corpora delictorum* I knew personally the one that lingers most persistently in my memory is the late Herman Rosenthal."[23] To Woollcott, the bloodiness and brutality of this murder served as an index to all those he had not witnessed but which he felt he could reconstruct by reference to the unforgettable visual details that remained with him from those few moments on the sidewalk: "I shall always remember that soft, fat body wilting on the sidewalk, with a beer-stained tablecoth serving as its pall. I shall always remember the fish-belly faces of the silent crowd which, sprung from nowhere, formed like a clot around these clamorous wounds."[24]

By the time Woollcott had published *While Rome Burns*, he was widely considered an authority on murder lore, and the section of readings that he titled "It May Be Human Gore" appealed to readers as classic examples of the true murder tale. Besides "Murder for Publicity," this section contains an account of the ominous but unexplained disappearance of a Brooklyn spinster ("In Behalf of an Absentee"), along with a resume of the famous "bridge table murder" of 1929, in which a wife shot her husband twice in an argument over a bridge hand, for which "unfortunate accident" she was acquitted ("By the Rude Bridge"). Woollcott provides also a singularly full and entertaining account of the freeing of one Nan Patterson, a *Floradora* showgirl, from the charge of shooting her married lover while riding beside him in a horse-drawn cab ("The Mystery of the Hansom Cab"),[25] and a wry account of the way in which an unscrupulous newspaperman capitalized upon the case of "a precocious harlot from Augusta, Maine," whose young lover was acquitted of the charge of having murdered her with an ax and having set fire to her bed in a New York brothel ("La Belle Hélène and Mr. B.").

Before he died, Woollcott had prepared a similar section for *Long, Long Ago*, which the editors entitled "Ways That Are Dark." Here, under the subsection title of "Five Classic Crimes," he included his already widely acclaimed "miniaturized" or "capsule" accounts of the Hall-Mills case, the Hauptmann case, the Snyder-Gray case, the Elwell case, and the Wanderer case ("The Case of the Ragged Stranger"). Among "Ways That Are Dark" he also provided some longer accounts of other cases—the famous Archer-Shee case; a case of the maltreatment-murder of a half-witted girl by her husband, his mistress, his brother, and his sister-in-law—all for the little property she had inherited ("That Affair at Penge");[26] and a ghost story titled "Quite Immaterial."

By the early 1930s, Woollcott was so well known as a connoisseur of murder lore that playwright Russel Crouse asked him to write the preface to *Murder Won't Out* (1932), a compendium of twelve retold, unsolved murder stories from 1799 to 1931. Since Woollcott, who supported the theory that more murderers go free than are ever caught and successfully brought to justice, had suggested this book to Crouse, he willingly wrote a preface full of illustrations that gave weight and credence to Crouses's title. To Woollcott, however, the ultimate honor of this sort was a request from the Modern Library that he provide the Foreword for their combined edition of Wilkie Collins's *The Moonstone* and *The Woman in White* (1937).

Long a public banner bearer for *The Moonstone* as a pioneer classic in the detective novel category, Woollcott now took great satisfaction in pointing out that "it is a curious phenomenon of letters that the first full-length detective novel ever written in any language should not yet have been surpassed or even equalled."[27] He seized this opportunity to castigate publishers for delaying the deserved acceptance of Collins by reproducing his two novels in execrably small print and in unsatisfactory abridgements. Moreover, he complained bitterly that Forster, the biographer of Dickens, had been so jealous of Collins as to ignore all the material that would have chronicled the close friendship of these two writers. In his petty spite, Forster had thereby deprived Dorothy L. Sayers of the essential material for a Collins biography that for at least seven years Woollcott had been urging her to finish.[28]

In his *Second Reader*, Woollcott gives ample evidence of the importance that the murder and mystery tale had assumed among his own literary tastes, for three substantial selections in this anthology belong to that genre. In reprinting Edith Wharton's "The Lady's Maid's Bell," he mentions also her warning that the radio and the movies had almost destroyed modern man's capacity to enjoy the written ghost story.[29] In his afterword to William Austin's "Peter Rugg, The Missing Man," he revealed that, though the story had become virtually a part of American folklore, it had actually first been invented by a Massachusetts lawyer. And he pointed out that William Bolitho's "The Self-Help of G. J. Smith" had been originally published in a book that Woollcott never hesitated to acknowledge as a classic of its kind, *Murder for Profit*.

CHAPTER 8

Quietus

I F the dramatic criticism and the popular belletristic works of Alexander Woollcott have never quite found their way into the mainstream of American letters, Woollcott's career as a writer has remained highly significant in many ways. The history of dramatic criticism in America owes much to Woollcott's courageous stand against the severe and autocratic control by which theater managers had traditionally "purchased" the services of the critics and by which management had made a mockery of their integrity as writers and arbiters. Under Woollcott's leadership and example, moreover, dramatic reviewing lost its Classical pretensions and became one of the "modern" literary forms. As a result, Woollcott was the most powerful single force responsible for ushering in the "great era" of dramatic criticism in America.

Though theater people quailed at the prospect of damnation by the sly and devastating tone of Woollcott's reviews, he loved the theater inordinately and drew his deepest satisfaction from the praises he could lavish. The theater was "always his love, his sweet, his ladye faire,"[1] wrote Dorothy Parker; and despite his constant effort to write the most carefully balanced of estimates, his native enthusiasm for plays and performers made him the premier practitioner of "appreciative" criticism in the twentieth century.

Because Woollcott had an abiding fascination with the people of the theater, he sought them out, befriended them, cultivated them, learned at first hand the intimate details of their lives and their art—and he thereby opened up new worlds of dramatic criticism by rejecting the ancient professional fiat against a critic's consorting with stage folk. Again, it was his devoted friend Dorothy Parker who remarked that Woollcott "has, I should think, between seven and eight hundred intimate friends, with all of whom he converses only in terms of atrocious insult."[2] Though she was using deliberate

152

hyperbole, Woollcott's voracious capacity for collecting people led him away from the immediate world of the theater and into the world of the universal raconteur.

As an essayist and a tale teller, Woollcott was unique. In the history of American letters, the publication of *While Rome Burns* has been a neglected landmark—the appearance in the twentieth century of several varieties of belles-lettres that had been highly respected in Old World cultures but that had not held an important place in American literature since the days of Irving and Hawthorne. This book "marked the emergence of a form new to the period: the smooth art of the raconteur-essayist: a sort of twentieth-century *Colloquia*,"[3] observed Samuel Hopkins Adams. Moreover, it is fitting that the stylistic sophistication of this volume won for Woollcott a place among the literati, even though American literature has seldom accepted the "pure" tale teller or the creator of informal *colloquia* among its major figures.

Had the development of the American literary tradition made a place in its mainstream for the stylist *qua* stylist, Woollcott would not have been overlooked among the top contenders for that position. Having decided that he was "a great writer with nothing to say,"[4] he elevated the art of saying to its highest estate, and he developed his own inimitable methods for achieving the leisurely and graceful but deceptive indirectness that has always been the distinguishing characteristic of the familiar essay and its allied forms. In this particular, Woollcott is supreme among American essayists, as John Mason Brown was suggesting, among other things, when he said that Woollcott's technique "was to beckon us down by-paths to reach a by-path. Yet all the while he is able to give us the illusion of having travelled the main road or the sense of relief that comes from having avoided it."[5] Like most of the critics and men of letters who wrote of Woollcott at the time of his death or shortly after it, Brown was convinced that Woollcott was assured of a respectable niche somewhere in American literary history.

There is something about the prolific production of periodical literature, however, that militates against the permanence of a literary reputation, no matter how high the quality of an author's best work might be. Though Woollcott achieved unprecedented popularity as a result of his uncanny rapport with the vast and faceless common reader of his day, he too often wrote for the common reader at the expense of the approval of the discriminating reader who would eventually judge his worth by other standards. The common reader of that day reveled in Woollcott's prolific revival of the school of sentiment and in his retelling of the world's great crime stories, but the discriminating reader of a later generation perceives that sentiment is a minor emotion and that the retelling of old murders appeals only to the sensations. Neither of these contributions is "original" in any sense that the discriminating reader is willing to credit highly. Therefore, though most critics prefer to judge a writer by his best work, the sheer bulk of Woollcott's popular literature has made it almost impossible for his best work to prevail.

For these reasons, Woollcott's most important contributions to dramatic criticism and belles–lettres have been obscured and overlooked, as has one other of his unique accomplishments: his impact upon the development of the whole field of "communications" in America. During the early, formative years of radio broadcasting, he brought to the airwaves a sense of personality—of flair and maturity—in a mass medium that had been too busily growing to develop any distinguishing character of its own. "Perhaps Mr. Woollcott's greatest gift to radio, over a period of years, was style," wrote John K. Hutchens, who went on to observe that "in the slightest of the Woollcott programs there was style, the conscientious writer's care for the exact word, for balance and mood and structure."[6] And this quality of Woollcott's prose continues to impress readers. "Woollcott knew words the way a diamond-buyer with a loupe in his eye recognizes a new stone,"[7] observed Howard Teichmann as recently as 1976.

But in the field of "communications," Woollcott did not stop with radio. He wrote and acted in plays; he worked with the movies; and he was one of the most widely sought and highly remunerated platform lecturers of his era. At a time before it became a general movement for American colleges and universities to establish departments or schools of "communications," Woollcott had already declared as part of his professional credo that "there is some merit . . . for any journalist to use each medium available in his time."[8] As a result, Alexander Woollcott's talents were almost incredibly versatile. "Never had there been a conversationalist, a jester, a storyteller, a critic of theater and literature such as he" writes Teichmann. "Nor has there been anyone to succeed him in the thirty-odd years since his death."[9]

Yet, in all that Woollcott said or wrote, he is most remarkable for his inimitable style; and in the years since his death, most of the estimates of his contributions to American literature arrive at the general conclusion that Woollcott will be read for his style if he is read at all. Looking back upon Woollcott's career at the time of the posthumous publication of *Long, Long Ago*, Ben Ray Redman declared, "he had a style, or the truth may be that the style had him."[10] During his own lifetime he was listed as a "best-selling personality" along with Sinclair Lewis, T. E. Lawrence, and Anne Lindbergh,[11] and when he was parodied in the mock retelling of a nursery rhyme, his style was set beside that of William Faulkner.[12] Even those who recognize the limitations of Woollcott's art have been willing to predict for it a longevity that has not materialized in the years since Woollcott's death. Instead, there has been a puzzling and an unfortunate quietus that suggests that the American literary tradition has not yet accepted Odell Shepard's prediction that, though Woollcott made stories out of anecdotes, "there is a finish and finality about them that promises long life."[13]

The Woollcott legend has enjoyed a long life, but the finish and the finality of his remarkable prose has yet to be given its due.

Notes and References

Chapter One

1. There are some signs of renewed interest in Woollcott. Frank Sullivan, a friend of Woollcott from the early 1920s, writes that he has recently heard of "considerable interest in Woollcott among young college men." These reports came from his godson at Harvard and from a recent graduate of Dartmouth (Letter to Wayne Chatterton from Sullivan, August 30, 1971).) Moreover, in his recent Woollcott biography, *Smart Aleck* (New York, 1976), pp. 9–10, Howard Teichmann is gratified by the widespread interest in Woollcott that young people still demonstrate.

2. Edwin Palmer Hoyt, *Alexander Woollcott: The Man Who Came to Dinner* (London and New York, 1968), p. 1.

3. Letter to Wayne Chatterton from E.B. White, July 29, 1971.

4. John Mason Brown, "Introduction," *The Portable Woollcott* (New York, 1946), p. xx.

5. Samuel Hopkins Adams, *A. Woollcott; His Life and His World* (New York, 1945), p. 1.

6. "Required Reading for Meatless Days," in *Long, Long Ago* (New York, 1943), p. 31.

7. Adams, p. 3.

8. Letter to Wayne Chatterton from Frank Sullivan, August 30, 1971.

9. Letter to Wayne Chatterton from Edwin P. Hoyt, September 29, 1971.

10. Edmund Wilson, "Alexander Woollcott of the Phalanx," in *Classics and Commercials; A Literary Chronicle of the Forties* (New York, 1950), p. 87.

11. See the explanation of these concepts by Nicholas V. Riasanovsky, *The Teaching of Charles Fourier* (Berkeley and Los Angeles, 1969), pp. 210–12.

12. E. S. Mason, "Fourier and Anarchism," *The Quarterly Journal of Economics*, XLII, 2 (February 1928), 260.

13. According to accounts by some of the biographers, Aleck's mother and sister Julie had been reading *Bleak House*, and his mother secretly

157

passed a note to Julie containing the quotation. For Woollcott's own accounts, see *Letters of Alexander Woollcott,* ed. Beatrice Kaufman and Joseph Hennessey (Garden City, New York; 1944), pp. 81 and 109.

14. "I Might Just as Well Have Played Hooky," in *Long, Long Ago,* p. 176.

15. "Perfectly Gone," in *Long, Long Ago,* p. 251.

16. "Hoof-beats on a Bridge," in *Long, Long Ago,* p. 167.

17. Hoyt, p. 51.

18. Adams, p. 53.

19. *Ibid.*

20. "What the Doctor Ordered," in *Long, Long Ago,* p. 240.

21. Hoyt, p. 116.

22. Adams, p. 99.

23. Issue of February 1921. The reprint used here is in *The Magic Mirror. Selected Writings on the Theatre by George Jean Nathan,* ed. Thomas Quinn Curtiss (New York, 1960), pp. 64–74.

24. "Four Best-Selling Personalities," *The Literary Digest,* CXXI (January 11, 1936), 28.

25. Frank Case, *Tales of a Wayward Inn* (New York, 1938), p. 60.

26. Adams, p. 119.

27. Corey Ford, *The Time of Laughter* (Boston, 1967), pp. 106–107.

28. Quoted in *News-Week* (October 13, 1934), p. 26.

29. Adams, p. 108.

30. Letter from Woollcott to Lilly Bonner, *Letters,* p. 100.

31. George S. Kaufman and Moss Hart, "The Man Who Came to Dinner," in *Si.: Plays by Kaufman and Hart* (New York, 1942), pp. 404–505.

32. In my interview with Marc Connelly, Mr. Connelly opened the discussion with this interesting understatement: "Aleck Woollcott was a most proprietary fellow."

33. Anon., *The New Republic,* CVIII (February 1, 1943), 135 (an obituary).

34. Harrison Smith, "Appreciation," *The Saturday Review of Literature,* XII (February 6, 1943), 12.

35. For an intimate fictionalized view of life at Neshobe during these years, s ·e Charles Brackett's novel *Entirely Surrounded* (New York, 1934). Brackett was a frequent visitor at the island, and most of the real life celebrities can be easily recognized in Brackett's characters.

36. Letter to Wayne Chatterton from Frank Sullivan, Aug. 30, 1971.

37. Adams, p. 2.

38. "The World of A. Woollcott," *The Reader's Digest,* XLII (May 1943), 9.

39. John Mason Brown, "That Other Alexander," *The Saturday Review of Literature,* XXVIII (June 23, 1945), 28. Teichmann, however, appears to disagree with many of these assessments. During my telephone conversa-

tion with him on August 3, 1977, Teichmann suggested that Woollcott was not as complex a personality as he seemed.

40. Booth Tarkington, "Ave Atque Vale, A. W.," *Atlantic Monthly,* CLXXI (June 1943), 64.

41. Adams, "World of A. Woollcott," 13.

42. Smith, p. 12.

43. Interview by Wayne Chatterton with Marc Connelly at his Park West apartment in New York City, August 17, 1971.

Chapter Two

1. Brown, Introduction, p. xii.

2. *Hamilton Literary Magazine,* XL (December 1905), 126–32.

3. *Hamilton Literary Magazine,* XL (February 1906), 212–20.

4. Of the five *Bohemian* magazines that came and went during several decades in America, only the one at Deposit, New York, was in operation at the time Woollcott wrote and submitted his story. See Albert Parry, *Garrets and Pretenders; A History of Bohemianism in America* (New York, 1960), pp. 261–65. A revision of the 1933 edition, with a new chapter by Harry T. Moore.

5. *Hamilton Literary Magazine,* XL (January 1906), 185–86.

6. *Hamilton Literary Magazine,* XLIII (June 1908), 20–30.

7. *Hamilton Literary Magazine,* XLI (November 1906), 79–82.

8. Hoyt (p. 42) says that Billy asks this question and gets this reply. But Pearl actually carries on this repartee with Crenshaw.

9. *Hamilton Literary Magazine,* XLI (April 1907), 261–69.

10. *Hamilton Literary Magazine,* XL (April 1906), 295–302.

11. *Hamilton Literary Magazine,* XLII (February 1908), 215–27.

12. *Hamilton Literary Magazine,* XL (October 1905), 54–56.

13. *Hamilton Literary Magazine,* XLII (November 1907), 101–05.

14. Edna Ferber once encouraged Woollcott to write novels, but he firmly refused. See Hoyt, p. 146.

15. Charles Angoff, "The Library: Alexander Woollcott," *The American Mercury,* LXI (August 1945), 242.

16. Adams, "The World of A. Woollcott," p. 13.

17. *Enchanted Aisles* (New York and London, 1924), pp. 82–87.

18. *While Rome Burns* (New York, 1934), pp. 229–32.

19. *Ibid.,* pp. 101–106.

20. From Paris, July 16, 1918; *Letters,* p. 62.

21. Brown, "That Other Alexander," p. 30.

22. Hoyt, p. 114.

23. Bennett Cerf, "Woollcott, A Minority Report," *The American Mercury,* LIX (August 1944), 174.

24. Adams, *A. Woollcott,* p. 90.

25. *Letters*, p. 62.

26. See Calder M. Pickett, "A Paper for the Doughboys: *Stars and Stripes* in World War I," *The Journalism Quarterly*, XLII (Winter 1965), 65–66.

27. *Verdun Belle* (New York, 1928), pp. 73–91.

28. John T. Winterich, *Squads Write!* (New York and London, 1931), pp. 63–64. See also Winterich's account of the circumstances under which Woollcott first got the story of Verdun Belle, pp. 60–63. Winterich and Woollcott were on assignment together at the time.

29. Brown Introduction, p. xxiv.

30. *Ibid.*, p. xix.

31. Danton Walker, "The Man Who Came to Dinner," *Theatre Arts*, XXXV (January 1951), 96.

Chapter Three

1. Carr Van Anda, quoted by Adams, *A. Woollcott*, p. 65.

2. Letter to Wayne Chatterton from Edwin P. Hoyt, September 29, 1971.

3. See Brooks Atkinson, (New York, 1940) *Broadway*, pp. 157–59.

4. "Bitter Memories," in *Shouts and Murmurs* (New York, 1922), p. 96. This essay was originally one of the "Second Thoughts," New York *Times*, April 11, 1920.

5. "Bitter Memories," p. 97.

6. "Second Thoughts," New York *Times*, October 3, 1920, p. 1.

7. "The Play," New York *Times*, October 21, 1919, p. 13.

8. Hoyt, p. 65.

9. Jerry Stagg, *The Brothers Shubert* (New York, 1968), pp. 114–17.

10. The American theater and its public have always demonstrated a special fondness for the courtroom drama. Only a few years after his own court battle, Woollcott observed that "the American stage may show signs of strain in its efforts to present a ball-room but it can be trusted to do a courtroom to perfection, and it has had a lot of practice." "The Play," New York *Times*, April 5, 1921, p. 24.

11. New York *Times*, April 11, 1915, p. 12.

12. New York *Times*, April 16, 1915, p. 13.

13. New York *Times*, May 19, 1915, p. 13.

14. See "Injunction Entered Against Shuberts," New York *Times*, May 25, 1915, p. 15; and "Shuberts Appeal Order," New York *Times*, June 10, 1915, p. 7.

15. New York *Times*, June 19, 1915, p. 9.

16. New York *Times*, July 10, 1915, p. 7.

17. Quoted in New York *Times*, November 18, 1915, p. 16.

18. New York *Times*, April 14, 1915, p. 7.

19. See "Government Seeks a Theatrical Trust," "May Reach Theatre Trust," and "Theatre Managers Must Show Books" in New York *Times* for April 7, p. 1; April 8, p. 9; April 9, p. 11.

20. New York *Times*, April 10, 1915, p. 11.

21. See New York *Times*, "Critic Vs. Managers," April 18, 1915, p. 1; "A Service to Criticism," April 25, 1915, p. 2; "The Ancient Feud," May 7, 1915, p. 12; "The Critic's Unhappiness," May 27, 1915, p. 10; and "Theatrical Goods," June 1, 1915, p. 14.

22. New York *Times*, June 8, 1915, p. 13.

23. Stagg, p. 137.

Chapter Four

1. Cerf, p. 175.

2. E. B. White, who read Woollcott's *Times* columns regularly during the 1920s, feels that Woollcott was especially effective as a writer of reviews. Writing to me on August 9, 1971, White made this useful observation: "There is, of course, a distinction between criticism and reviewing, and Woollcott was essentially a reviewer: he could attend an opening, leave the theater for a nearby typewriter, and within an hour or so produce a lively and concise account of what he had seen—for consumption at breakfast the next morning when you opened your paper. What I remember best about his reviews was that he almost always left me knowing whether or not I wanted to see the play. Also, they were fun to read."

3. "The Play," New York *Times*, December 24, 1920, p. 14.

4. Any lists, general observations, or summarized materials concerning Woollcott's drama columns in the *Times* have been derived from an examination of complete copies of "The Play" and "Second Thoughts on First Nights" as these columns appeared in that newspaper from 1915 to 1922 when Woollcott left the *Times* for the *Herald*. Specific references to these columns will be cited according to the individual column in which the information appears and to the date of the issue.

5. "The Play," December 23, 1919, p. 12.

6. "Second Thoughts," April 18, 1920, p. 2.

7. "The Play," November 26, 1919, p. 11.

8. "Second Thoughts," November 30, 1919, p. 2.

9. "Second Thoughts," December 11, 1921, p. 1.

10. "Second Thoughts," October 3, 1920, p. 1. Though Woollcott distrusted list making, he regularly compiled various lists of "bests" and "worsts" at the demand of his public.

11. "Second Thoughts," December 14, 1919, p. 2.

12. "The Play," March 1, 1921, p. 18.

13. "Second Thoughts," November 9, 1919, p. 2.

14. "Second Thoughts," April 4, 1920, p. 6.

15. "Second Thoughts," November 13, 1921, p. 1.

16. "The Play," November 3, 1921, p. 22. Later, however, he became irritated by O'Neill's "artistic intransigeance" and made the mistake of attacking *Strange Interlude* from his reading of a preproduction script, whereupon relations between the playwright and the critic became distant. Atkinson, p. 252.

17. "The Play," April 27, 1921, p. 21.

18. "Second Thoughts," February 1, 1920, p. 2.

19. "Second Thoughts," October 5, 1919, p. 2.

20. Among the most feared of the daily reviewers in New York at this time were Percy Hammond and Heywood Broun. According to Adams (*A. Woollcott*, p. 114), "Both . . . were, like Woollcott, gross of waistline. The profession dubbed them 'The Three Fat Fates of Broadway.' "

21. "The Play," October 12, 1920, p. 18.

22. "The Play," March 2, 1920, p. 9.

23. "The Play," March 22, 1921, p. 15.

24. "The Play," February 18, 1920, p. 9.

25. "Second Thoughts," April 18, 1920, p. 2.

26. "The Play," March 1, 1920, p. 16.

27. "Second Thoughts," April 11, 1920, p. 2.; also included later as part of "Bitter Memories" in *Shouts and Murmurs*, p. 100.

28. "Second Thoughts," December 4, 1921, p. 1.

29. *Shouts and Murmurs* p. 105.

30. "Second Thoughts," December 4, 1921, p. 1.

31. "Second Thoughts," October 17, 1915, p. 8.

32. "Second Thoughts," October 24, 1915, p. 6.

33. "Second Thoughts," November 14, 1920, p. 1.

34. "Second Thoughts," January 9, 1921, p. 1.

35. "Second Thoughts," April 24, 1921, p. 1.

36. "Second Thoughts," May 1, 1921, p. 1.

37. Atkinson, p. 212.

38. "Second Thoughts," December 19, 1915, p. 8.

39. "The Play," November 11, 1920, p. 11.

40. "Second Thoughts," November 21, 1920, p. 1.

41. "Second Thoughts," December 12, 1920, p. 1.

42. "Second Thoughts," December 18, 1921, p. 1.

43. "Second Thoughts," October 5, 1919, p. 2.

44. This was before the day of the "instant star" of the Hollywood variety, but it is unlikely that Woollcott would have considered the Hollywood phenomenon as legitimate stardom in the sense of his definition.

45. "Second Thoughts," October 17, 1920, p. 1.

46. "Born of Strolling Players," in *Shouts and Murmurs*, p. 44.

47. "Second Thoughts," May 15, 1921, p. 1.

48. "The Play," October 19, 1920, p. 12.

49. "The Play," April 8, 1921, p. 18.

50. "The Play," February 18, 1920, p. 9.

51. "The Play," December 2, 1919, p. 11.

52. "The Play," December 24, 1920, p. 14.

53. See for example "The Play," April 20, 1921, p. 11; May 3, 1921, p. 20; May 14, 1921, p. 10.

54. Margaret Case Harriman says that the actors at the scattered tables in the Algonquin were not particularly interested in what was going on at the Round Table—except for those who were "terrified of Alexander Woollcott's reviews." *The Vicious Circle* (New York, 1951), pp. 32–33.

55. "The Play," December 16, 1919, p. 18.

56. "The Play," January 14, 1920, p. 12.

57. "The Play," October 21, 1919, p. 13.

58. "The Play," November 16, 1920, p. 19.

59. "The Play," November 2, 1920, p. 15.

60. "The Play," April 8, 1921, p. 18.

61. "Second Thoughts," October 30, 1921, p. 1.

62. "The Play," December 31, 1919, p. 5.

63. "The Play," April 2, 1921, p. 14. Woollcott was an ingenious and sometimes an uncontrollable punster. At Hamilton, having discovered his supremacy in this peculiar sort of wordplay, he apparently specialized in puns that were ribald if not "raw"—probably for the sake of the attention he thereby commanded. During his early years as a *Times* reviewer, his editors had to keep close watch on his copy to eliminate what Adams (*A. Woollcott*, p. 71) calls "the crypto-pun on familiar four-letter words." Among the Algonquin Wits, however, a well-turned pun was considered a form of "wisecrack," and few of the "Wits" could survive a punning contest against Woollcott. Therefore, Woollcott could rarely resist the temptation to take advantage of an ingenious pun in his writing. The headline for a "Second Thoughts" might be "A Playful Week." He describes a trite play as "a long and quenching draft from the old hokum bucket." And when he observed the expensive wall hangings in the new Guild Theater, he warned, "The Gobelins will get you if you don't watch out."

64. "The Play," October 5, 1920, p. 12.

65. "The Play," December 24, 1921, p. 7.

66. "Second Thoughts," November 21, 1915, p. 8.

67. "Second Thoughts," April 25, 1920, p. 2; and December 12, 1920, p. 1.

68. "Second Thoughts," October 23, 1921, p. 1.

69. "The Play," November 11, 1920, p. 11.

70. "The Play," May 12, 1921, p. 20.

71. Hoyt, pp. 138–39.

72. See Marc Connelly, *Voices Offstage* (New York, 1968), pp. 83–89; and Howard Teichmann, *George S. Kaufman an Intimate Portrait* (New

York, 1972), pp. 73–74. For reference to Benchley's "Treasurer's Report," both Nathaniel Benchley, *Robert Benchley* (New York, 1955), pp. 153–55, and Babette Rosmond, *Robert Benchley, His Life and Good Times* (New York, 1970), pp. 93–99, tell the story and provide the full text of the "Report."

73. See Walton R. Patrick, *Ring Lardner* (New York, 1963), pp. 137–40.

74. Taylor's remark appeared in Woollcott's essay "A Few Annoying Dramas," *Enchanted Aisles*, p. 196.

75. Woollcott points out that the performance of "The Survival of the Fittest" elicited Heywood Broun's near classic description of the hero's acting: "Mr. Love's idea of playing a he-man," said Mr. Broun, "was to extend his chest three inches and then follow it slowly across the stage."

76. Letter from Woollcott to Lynn Fontanne, September 25, 1934, *Letters*, p. 36.

77. Adams, A. *Woollcott*, p. 156.

Chapter Five

1. *Letters*, p. 286.

2. *Shouts and Murmurs*, p. 143.

3. In this chapter all parenthetical page numbers in the text refer to pages in the Woollcott book being discussed in that section—i.e., all such numbers in Section I refer to *Mrs. Fiske;* in Section II they refer to *Mr. Dickens Goes to the Play.*

4. "The Modern Theatre and Its Problems," New York *Times* Book Review, December 30, 1917, p. 578.

5. "Best Books of the Year as Selected by a National Jury of Critics," *Current Opinion*, LXIII (December 1917), 414–15.

6. T. E. Pemberton, *Dickens and the Stage* (London, 1888); and A. J. A. Fitzgerald, *Dickens and the Drama* (London, 1910).

7. "Dickens and the Theatre," New York *Times* Book Review, December 3, 1922, p. 4.

8. F. J. H. Danton, *Vincent Crummles: His Theatre and His Times* (New York, 1926); and J. B. Van Amerongen, *The Actor in Dickens* (1927; rpt. New York and London, 1969).

9. Clayton Hamilton, *Literary Review* (December 9, 1922), 228.

10. "The Editor Recommends—," *The Bookman*, LVI (November 1922), 339.

11. Letter of Woollcott to Jerome Kern, July 1924, *Letters*, p. 77.

12. Louis Kronenberger, "Irving Berlin, 'From Rags to Riches,' " New York *Times* Book Review, April 12, 1925, p. 11.

13. Cohan said this when he introduced Berlin at a meeting of the Friar's Club. Woollcott quotes part of Cohan's speech in *The Story of Irving Berlin* (New York and London, 1925), p. 95.

14. The book is to a large extent the story of the rise of the Russian Jew in America—not only of Berlin but also of Eddie Cantor, Al Jolson, and several others of lesser fame.

15. Mark Van Doren, "First Glance," *The Nation*, CXX (May 20, 1925), 574.

16. Douglas Moore, "On Irving Berlin," *The Saturday Review of Literature*, I (June 13, 1925), 823.

17. John Farrar, "Intimate Biography," *The Bookman*, LXI (May 1925), 345.

18. Woollcott was only one of Kaufman's eighteen collaborators. See Howard Teichmann, "By George S. Kaufman and . . . ," The New York *Times Magazine*, November 13, 1966, pp. 64–87 *passim*.

19. Teichmann, *George S. Kaufman*, p. 31.

20. *Ibid.*, p. 97.

21. A. Mccs. S., *Catholic World*, CXX (December 1929), 333–34.

22. Joseph Wood Krutch, *The Nation*, CXXIX (November 6, 1929), 530.

23. Brooks Atkinson, "The Play," New York *Times*, October 18, 1929, p. 1.

24. Brooks Atkinson, "The Open Season," New York *Times*, October 27, 1929, p. 1.

25. Francis R. Bellamy, "The Theatre," *Outlook and Independent*, CLIII (November 6, 1929), 389.

26. John Hutchens, "In Many Moods," *Theatre Arts Magazine*, XIII (December 1929), 881.

27. Richard Dana Skinner, "The Play," *Commonweal*, XXI (December 8, 1933), 19.

28. Brooks Atkinson, "The Play," New York *Times*, November 27, 1933, p. 20.

29. "Theatre Arts Bookshelf. Plays in Print," *Theatre Arts Monthly*, XVIII (May 1934), 390.

Chapter Six

1. Wolcott Gibbs, "Big Nemo," in *More in Sorrow* (New York, 1958) p. 109.

2. Adams, *A. Woollcott*, p. 256.

3. Letter to Wayne Chatterton from E. B. White, September 27, 1971.

4. James Thurber, *The Years with Ross* (Boston, 1959), p. 277.

5. Gibbs, p. 114.

6. Thurber, p. 276.

7. To Arnold Gingrich, Woollcott's voice sounded "oily" over the telephone.

8. Samuel Hopkins Adams, "Alexander Woollcott, Town Crier," *Harper's Magazine*, CXC (February 1945), 269.

9. John Hutchens, "The Late Town Crier," New York *Times* Radio Page, January 31, 1943, p. 9.

10. Brown, "That Other Alexander," p. 44.

11. *Ibid.*, p. 31.

12. Unpublished letter of Woollcott to John Gielgud in Houghton Library collection, Harvard University, dated December 4, 1936.

13. David H. Beetle, "Lavender and Old Torsos, A Report on the Woollcott Library," *Harper's Magazine*, CLXXXVIII (May 1944), 500.

14. "The Deep-Tangled Kaufman," *The New Yorker*, V (May 18, 1929), 33–36. "The Two-Eyed Connelly," VI (April 12, 1930), 29–32; "Portrait of a Man With Red Hair," *The New Yorker*, IV (December 1, 1928), 33–36.

15. Joseph Mersand included this essay in his *Great American Short Biographies* (New York, 1966). Moreover, Woollcott reprinted it in *Long, Long Ago* as he did the essay upon Lord Jeffrey Amherst, "A Soldier of the King."

16. Sharon Brown, *Present Tense* (New York, 1947), pp. 487–93.

17. "Annie Sullivan," *Atlantic*, CLXIII (March 1939), 305–308; Cornelia Lunt," *Atlantic*, CLXIV (April 1939), 466–69; "Ira Dutton," *Atlantic*, CLXIII (June 1939), 805–808; "Rose Field," *Atlantic*, CLXIII (May 1939), 643–48.

18. The essays on Miss Lunt and Ira Dutton appeared in *Long, Long Ago* under the respective titles of "The Old, The Young, and the Ageless" and "The Green Mountain Boys." He also includes a moving tribute to J. M. Barrie, "in memory of one who is close now to the end of his journey," p. 218.

19. Edward Weeks, "The Atlantic Bookshelf," *Atlantic Monthly*, CLXII (December 1943), 133.

20. Odell Shepard, "The Art of Story-Telling," *The Yale Review*, XXV (Spring 1936), 648.

21. John Mason Brown, "Mr. Woollcott Comes for Dinner," in *Broadway in Review* (New York, 1940), p. 89.

22. Otis Ferguson, "Man About Town," *The New Republic*, LXXIX (May 30, 1934), 79.

Chapter Seven

1. Brown, "That Other Alexander," pp. 39–40.

2. "Foreword," *Woollcott's Second Reader* (New York, 1937), p. ix.

3. "Shouts and Murmurs," *The New Yorker*, X (May 5, 1934), 39.

4. Woollcott's earlier version of the legend appeared in "Shouts and Murmurs," *The New Yorker*, VI (March 1, 1930), 32, under the title of "Histoire de France."

5. In *While Rome Burns*, this account appears under the section heading of "Century of Progress."

6. "Shouts and Murmurs," *The New Yorker*, VI (June 14, 1930), 32.

7. "Shouts and Murmurs," *The New Yorker*, VI (April 26, 1930), 32.

8. "The Hidden House," *The Reader's Digest*, XLII (February 1943), 101–102.

9. Loring Holmes Dodd, *Celebrities at Our Hearthside* (Boston, 1959), p. 75.

10. Leonard Bacon, "The Juice of the Tenderized Prune," *Saturday Review of Literature*, X (March 17, 1934), 553.

11. Brown, "Mr. Woollcott Comes for Dinner," p. 89.

12. De Quincey's essay "Murder Considered As One of the Fine Arts," appeared originally in *Blackwood's* in two parts (1827 and 1829). From De Quincey's argument that murder and mirth are naturally allied come most of the later attempts to write lightly or flippantly of murder. Woollcott knew the essay well and referred to it frequently. See for instance "Shouts and Murmurs," *The New Yorker*, V (November 2, 1929), 42.

13. "The President's Crime Shelf," *Cosmopolitan* (April 1941), 42–43.

14. Adams, *A. Woollcott* p. 252.

15. In "Shouts and Murmurs," *The New Yorker*, V (August 31, 1929), 38, he referred to Lizzie Borden as "that inscrutable maiden of our own Fall River, whom British delvers in criminal lore have ever done us the honor to envy us."

16. Beetle, "Lavender and Old Torsos," p. 500.

17. "Shouts and Murmurs," *The New Yorker*, X (April 14, 1934), 38.

18. "Shouts and Murmurs," *The New Yorker*, V (February 31, 1930), 28.

19. "Shouts and Murmurs," *The New Yorker*, V (August 31, 1929), 38.

20. "Shouts and Murmurs," *The New Yorker*, V (October 5, 1929), 42.

21. "Shouts and Murmurs," *The New Yorker*, VI (July 12, 1930), 31. Reprinted in *While Rome Burns*.

22. "Shouts and Murmurs," *The New Yorker*, VI (August 2, 1930), 28.

23. "Shouts and Murmurs," *The New Yorker*, V (November 2, 1929), 42. A week later (November 9, p. 43), he devoted another page to exposing little-known sidelights of the Rosenthal case.

24. Foreword to Russel Crouse, *Murder Won't Out* (Garden City, New York; 1932), p. v. The first two paragraphs of this essay, including these lines, appeared later as the opening paragraphs of "La Belle Hélène and Mr. B." in *While Rome Burns*.

25. This tale first appeared in "Shouts and Murmurs," *The New Yorker*, May 3, 1930.

26. The original version of this account appeared in "Shouts and Murmurs," *The New Yorker*, March 24, 1934.

27. "Foreword" to Wilkie Collins, *The Moonstone and the Woman in White* (New York, 1937).

28. See "Shouts and Murmurs," *The New Yorker*, VI (May 24, 1930), 32.

29. See *Woollcott's Second Reader*, p. 32.

Chapter Eight

1. Dorothy Parker, "A Valentine for Mr. Woollcott," in *Vanity Fair. Selections from America's Most Memorable Magazine* (New York, 1960), p. 291.

2. *Ibid.*

3. Adams, A. *Woollcott*, p. 250.

4. *Ibid.*, p. 161.

5. Brown, "That Other Alexander," p. 41.

6. Hutchens, "The Late Town Crier," p. 9.

7. Teichmann, *Smart Aleck*, p. 198.

8. Letter from Woollcott to Laura E. Richards, December 9, 1940, *Letters*, p. 266.

9. Teichmann, *Smart Aleck*, p. 11.

10. Ben Ray Redman, "Woollcottian Variorum," *The Saturday Review of Literature*, XXVI (December 4, 1943), 4.

11. "Four Best-Selling Personalities," p. 28.

12. Timothy Fuller, "The Story of Jack and Jill As It Might Be Told by William Faulkner, P. G. Wodehouse, and Alexander Woollcott," *The Saturday Review of Literature*, XV (December 19, 1936), 10.

13. Shepard, p. 648.

Selected Bibliography

A complete bibliography of material by and about Woollcott has never been compiled, and it seems unlikely that the vast number of unindexed pieces by Woollcott will be located and listed within the foreseeable future. Although he wrote thousands of short pieces that cannot be listed here, all of his collections and a representative selection of the indexed materials appear in this bibliography. While reviews of his books are not included here, some important ones are fully documented in the Notes and References.

PRIMARY SOURCES

1. Books

The Command Is Forward. Tales of the A. E. F. Battlefields as They Appeared in "The Stars and Stripes." New York: The Century Co., 1919.

The Dark Tower. A Melodrama by Alexander Woollcott and George S. Kaufman. New York: Random House, 1934; New York and Los Angeles, S. French, 1937.

Enchanted Aisles. 2d ed., New York and London: G. P. Putnam's Sons, The Knickerbocker Press, 1924.

Going to Pieces. New York and London: G. P. Putnam's Sons, The Knickerbocker Press, 1928.

The Letters of Alexander Woollcott. Ed. Beatrice Kaufman and Joseph Hennessey. Garden City, New York: Garden City Publishing Co., Inc., 1944. Rprt., Viking Press Edition, 1947; Greenwood Press, 1975.

Long, Long Ago. New York: World Book Company Edition. Distributed by Viking Press, 1943.

Mrs. Fiske—Her Views on the Stage Recorded. New York: Benjamin Blom, Inc., 1968. Reissue of 1917 edition.

Mr. Dickens Goes to the Play. New York and London: G. P. Putnam's Sons, The Knickerbocker Press, 1922.

The Portable Woollcott. Selected by Joseph Hennessey, with an Introduction by John Mason Brown. "The Viking Portable Library." New York: The Viking Press, 1946; Rprt., Greenwood Press, 1975.

169

Shouts and Murmurs. Echoes of a Thousand and One First Nights. New York: The Century Co., 1922.
The Story of Irving Berlin. New York and London: G. P. Putnam's Sons, The Knickerbocker Press, 1925.
Two Gentlemen and a Lady. New York: Coward McCann, Inc., 1928.
Verdun Belle. Originally published under the title "Two Gentlemen and a Lady." New York: Grosset & Dunlap, Publishers, 1928.
While Rome Burns. 15th printing. New York: The Viking Press, 1935.

2. Books Edited by Woollcott

As You Were. A Portable Library of American Prose and Poetry Assembled for Members of the Armed Forces and the Merchant Marine. New York: The Viking Press, 1945.
The Woollcott Reader. Bypaths in the Realms of Gold. New York: The Viking Press, 1935; Deluxe ed., Garden City, New York: Garden City Publishing Company, Inc., 1938.
Woollcott's Second Reader. New York: The Viking Press, 1937.

3. Selected Articles and Stories Written by Woollcott for the Hamilton Literary Magazine

"An Old Dodge, or the Wisdom of Solomon." XL (January 1906), 185–86.
"The Bequest of the Golden Girl." XLIV (June 1909), 6.
"The Hand of the Potter." XLII (February 1908), 215–27.
"The Hearth and the Cloister." XL (December 1905), 126–32.
"Love-light." XLI (November 1906), 92.
"Paradise Lost." XLIII (June 1908), 20–30.
"Pearl." XLI (November 1906), 79–82.
"The Precipice." XL (February 1906), 212–20.
"The Swan Song." XL (April 1906), 295–302.
"Richard Mansfield." XLII (November 1907), 101–105.
"The Rushing of Timothy Starr." XLI (April 1907), 261–69.
"Two Novels: A Comparison." XL (October 1905), 54–56.

4. Articles and Stories by Woollcott in Periodicals and Newspapers

"Aladdin on Broadway." *Collier's*, LXXXI (February 18, 1928), 17, 32, 35.
"Author! Author!" *Collier's*, LXXVIII (September 4, 1926), 10, 44–45.
"Back in Brittany." *The North American Review*, CCXIII (March 1921), 362–70.
"Bobbed Hair; A Novel by Twenty Authors." *Collier's*, LXXV (January 10, 1925), 5–7, 32, 34–36.
"Brave Little Woman." *Collier's*, LXXIX (January 22, 1927), 10, 40.
"The Butter-and-egg Man." *Collier's*, LXXVII (April 17, 1926), 20–21.
"Charles Dickens, the Side-tracked Actor." *The North American Review*, CCXVI (October 1922), 513–22.

"The Child Actor Grows Up." *Everybody's Magazine*, XLII (February 1920), 57–58.

"The Child on the Garden Wall." *Collier's*, XXCIV (November 23, 1929), 14, 65.

"Disarming the Drama." *The Century*, CIX (October 1922), 841–43.

"The Dollar after Next." *Collier's*, LXXXVII (February 7, 1931), 10, 62.

"Dorothy Donnelly in a Double Role." *Pictorial Review*, XXVI (September 1925), 26, 113–14.

"Elmer, the Unexpected." *Collier's*, LXXXIII (May 4, 1929), 15, 66.

"Elsie Janis Capers on Western Front." The New York *Times*, June 17, 1918, p. 11.

"The Fleet and Brother Joseph." *The Reader's Digest*, XL (February 1942), 27–28.

" G. B. S. Forever: or Required Reading for Meatless Days." *Good Housekeeping*, CXV (December 1942), 21, 109.

"The Good Companions." *Cosmopolitan*, (August 1936), 42–43, 85–86; Rprt., *The Reader's Digest*, XXX (June 1937), 69–71.

"The Grand Old Man of the American Stage." *Everybody's Magazine*, XLII (March 1920), 59–60.

"The Guild of Peter Pans." *Everybody's Magazine*, XLIV (April 1921), 63.

"Harpo Smites His Lyre." *Collier's*, LXXXIV (July 20, 1929), 20, 45.

"Heywood Broun." *Bookman*, LIII (July 1921), 443.

"The Hidden House." *The Reader's Digest*, XLII (February 1943), 101–02.

"How a Critic Gets That Way." *Collier's*, LXXXI (February 25, 1928), 12, 44.

"How's It Look Over There?" *The North American Review*, CCXII (December 1920), 765–76.

"If You Could Go Back." *The Reader's Digest*, XXXIV (February 1937), 18–21.

"I'm Glad I'm Absent-minded." *The American Mercury Magazine*, CXIV (July 1932), 59–74, 76.

"Importing Tears and Laughter." *Everybody's Magazine*, XLIII (December 1920), 30–34.

"In Memoriam: Annie Sullivan." *The Atlantic Monthly*, CLXIII (March 1939), 305–308; Rprt., *The Reader's Digest*, XXXIV (May 1939), 68–71.

"In Memoriam: Cornelia Lunt." *The Atlantic Monthly*, CLXIV (April 1939), 466–69.

"In Memoriam: Ira Dutton." *The Atlantic Monthly*, CLXIII (June 1939), 805–808.

"In Memoriam: Rose Field." *The Atlantic Monthly*, CLXII (May 1939), 643–48; Rprt., *The Reader's Digest*, XXXIV (June 1939), 51–52.

"In Which We Serve." *The Reader's Digest*, XLII (March 1943), 94.

"The King Wasn't So Crazy." *Collier's*, LXXXV (January 4, 1930), 17, 45.

"The Knock at the Stage Door." *The North American Review*, CCXVI (September 1922), 378-84.

"The Last Mile." *Collier's,* LXXXV (May 3, 1930), 25, 64.

"Lessons between the Acts." *Collier's,* LXXXIV (August 31, 1929), 15, 30.

"The Long Run as a Curse." *Everybody's Magazine,* XLIV (May 1921), 26–27.

"The Miracle of the Stars and Stripes." *Everybody's Magazine,* XLII (January 1920), 61–68.

"Mrs. Fiske Builds a Theater in Spain." *The Century,* XCIII (April 1917), 909–18.

"Mrs. Fiske Goes to the Play." *The Century,* XCIV (May 1917), 71–82.

"Mrs. Fiske on Ibsen the Popular." *The Century,* XCIII (February 1917), 529–38.

"Mrs. Fiske to the Actor-in-the-Making." *The Century,* XCIII (March 1917), 714–23.

"Mrs. Fiske Punctures the Repertory Idea." *The Century,* XCIII (January 1917), 321–32.

"Murder at 8:30 Sharp." *Collier's,* LXXXI (March 17, 1928), 22, 49.

"My Seventh Assistant." *Good Housekeeping,* CXVI (May 1943), 44, 81.

"Oberammergau This Way." *Collier's,* LXXXVI (July 26, 1930), 16, 60–61.

"The Ordeal of Ben Ami." *Everybody's Magazine,* XLIV (March 1921), 64–65.

"A Partnership of the Theatre." *Everybody's Magazine,* XLII (May 1920), 78–79.

"The Play." The New York *Times,* 1915–1922. These columns were Woollcott's daily play reviews.

"The President's Crime Shelf." *Cosmopolitan,* (April 1941), 42–43, 119.

"Profiles: The Deep-tangled Kaufman." *The New Yorker,* V (May 18, 1929), 26–29.

"Profiles: Portrait of a Man with Red Hair." *The New Yorker,* IV (December 1928), 33–36.

"Profiles: The Two-Eyed Connelly." *The New Yorker,* VI (April 12, 1930), 29–32.

"The Quest of a Lost Childhood." *The Saturday Evening Post,* CC (April 7, 1928), 14–15, 157–58, 160.

"Reading and Writing," *McCall's* (beginning about 1930 through about 1934). This magazine is not indexed.

"The Rise of Eugene O'Neill." *Everybody's Magazine,* XLIII (July 1920), 49.

"The Rise of Swifty White." *Collier's,* LXXXI (May 19, 1928), 12, 49–50.

"Sally Farnham's Art." *The Delineator,* XCVIII (May 1921), 16.

"The Sandman's Magic." *Collier's,* LXXVII (January 30, 1926), 13, 45.

"Screen Credit for Emily Brontë." *The Ladies' Home Journal,* LVI (June 1939), 18, 119.

"The Second Hunt after the Captain." *The Atlantic Monthly,* CLXX (December 1942), 48–51.

"Second Thoughts on First Nights." The New York *Times*, 1915–1922. These columns were Woollcott's weekend thoughts on the plays he had reviewed during the week.

"She Didn't Mean to Do It." *Collier's*, LXXVIII (December 11, 1926), 11, 34.

"She Sounded Forth the Trumpet." St. Louis *Post-Dispatch*, March 22, 1942; Rprt., *The Reader's Digest*, XL (May 1942), 49–50.

"A Ship Comes In." *Collier's*, LXXXVII (April 11, 1931), 19, 56.

"Shouts and Murmurs." *The New Yorker*. A weekly page that ran from 1929 to 1934.

"Six Lessons in English." *The Reader's Digest*, XXXIV (February 1939), 92; (March 1939), 127; (April 1939), 129; (May 1939), 132; (June 1939), 107; (July 1939), 132. "Lessons in English," *The Reader's Digest*, XXXV (August 1939), 116; (September 1939), 80; (November 1939), 60; (December 1939), 104.

"Staged in Moscow." *Collier's*, XCII (December 16, 1933), 22, 46–47.

"Stars and Stripes." *The Saturday Evening Post*, CC (March 17, 1928), 3–5, 56 61–62; CC (March 24, 1928), 22–23, 157–58, 160–62, 165.

"A Stalwart Named Baldridge." *Bookman*, L (January 1920), 449–51.

"The Strenuous Honeymoon." *Everybody's Magazine*, XLIII (November 1920), 36–39.

"The Success of the Season." *The Century*, C (July 1920), 412–18.

"The Surprises of Abraham Lincoln." *Everybody's Magazine*, XLII (April 1920), 66–67.

"Them Damned Frogs." *North American Review*, CCX (October 1919), 490–98.

"To Loving Young People Apart." *The Reader's Digest*, XLI (December 1942), 1–2.

"Too Late to Mend." *Collier's*, LXXVIII (September 25, 1926), 26, 36.

"Twice Told Tales—I. Our Lady's Juggler." *The Reader's Digest*, XXXIX (October 1941), 15–16.

"Twice Told Tales—II. The Last Thing Shubert Wrote." *The Reader's Digest*, XXXIX (November 1941), 85–86.

"Twice Told Tales—III. The Fleet and Brother Joseph." *The Reader's Digest*, XL (February 1942), 27–28.

"The Two Barrymores." *Everybody's Magazine*, XLII (June 1920), 31.

"Up from Ten-twent'-thirt'." *Collier's*, LXXX (January 2, 1926), 7–8.

"Verdun Belle; A Story." *Collier's*, LXXX (October 22, 1927), 17.

"Victoria, Lizzie and Others." *Collier's*, LXXXV (April 19, 1930), 34, 43.

"Walt Whitman, Dramatic Critic." *Bookman*, LIII (March 1921), 75–77.

"What of It?" *The Reader's Digest*, XLI (July 1942), 85–86.

"What the Public Got." *Everybody's Magazine*, XLIV (June 1921), 42–43.

"White House Callers; With Grateful Acknowledgement to the Late Finley Peter Dunne." *The New Yorker*, XVII (March 15, 1941), 19.

"Who Is the Best Young American Actress?" *The Pictorial Review*, XXXII (April 1931), 2, 90, 92.

"The Woman Who Put Bolivar in Bronze." The New York *Times*, April 10, 1921, p. 25.

"Woollcott Presents." *The Saturday Review of Literature*, XVI (October 23, 1937), 13–14.

5. Woollcott in Anthologies, Novels, and Plays

"Capsule Criticism." *A Subtreasury of American Humor*, eds. E. B. White and Katharine S. White, pp. 534–39. New York: Coward-McCann, Inc., 1941.

"The Channel Road." *The Best Plays of 1929–1930*. ed. Burns Mantle, New York: Dodd, Mead and Company, 1930. p. 421.

"Colossal Bronze." *Present Tense*, ed. Sharon Brown, rev. ed., pp. 487–93. New York: Harcourt, Brace and Company, 1947.

"Dear Friends and Gentle Hearts." In *Great Modern American Short Biographies*, ed. and introduced by Joseph Mersand, pp. 86–91. New York: Dell Publishing Co., Inc., The Laurel-Leaf Library, 1966.

"Father Duffy." *Men at War. The Best War Stories of All Time*, ed. with an Introduction by Ernest Hemingway, pp. 981–83. New complete ed. New York: Bramhall House, 1955.

"Foreword." In Wilkie Collins, *The Moonstone and The Woman in White*, pp. v–viii. New York: The Modern Library, 1937.

"Foreword." In Gilda Varesi and Dolly Byrne, *Enter Madame*, pp. v–xiii. New York and London: G. P. Putnam's Sons, The Knickerbocker Press, 1921.

"Foreword." *Murder Won't Out*, ed. Russel Crouse, pp. v–viii. Garden City, New York: Doubleday, Doran & Company, Inc., 1932.

"Hands Across the Sea." In *Men at War. The Best War Stories of All Time*, ed. with an Introduction by Ernest Hemingway, pp. 931–33. New complete ed. New York: Bramhall House, 1955.

"In That State of Life." In *Modern American Prose*, ed. Carl Van Doren, pp. 889–94. New York: The Literary Guild; Harcourt, Brace and Company, Inc., 1934.

"Knight with a Rueful Countenance." In *Voices in Court; A Treasury of the Bench, Bar, and the Courtroom*, ed. William H. Davenport, pp. 71–77. New York: The Macmillan Company, 1958.

"Manhattan." In *A Subtreasury of American Humor*, ed. E. B. White and Katharine S. White, pp. 532–34. New York: Coward-McCann, Inc., 1941.

"No Yesterdays." In *Empire City; A Treasury of New York*, collected and edited by Alexander Klein, pp. 420–21. New York: Rinehart & Company, Inc., 1955.

"Profile: Portrait of a Man with Red Hair." In *Profiles from The New Yorker*. New York: Alfred A. Knopf, Inc., 1938.

6. Radio broadcasts

As Edwin P. Hoyt has said, most of the manuscripts of Woollcott's broadcasts are buried in a CBS warehouse in New Jersey, where they remain unavailable. Hoyt quotes many of the broadcasts in his biography, however, and the following are among those most readily available to interested readers.

"American Portrait." [Oliver Wendell Holmes] Broadcast October 28, 1941. Hamilton College Collection.
"Don't Shoot That Horse." Published in *The Reader's Digest*, XXX (June 1937), 13–14.
"For Us the Living; A Footnote to the Gettysburg Address." Recorded and published by Linguaphone Institute, Radio City, New York. [c. 1941]
Hamilton College Choir with Woollcott as M. C. CBS, March 6, 1938. Hamilton College Collection.
"Letters from America." NBC to the BBC, July 2, 1939. This series continued on July 9, 16, 23, 30 and August 6, 1939. Hamilton College Collection.
"The Town Crier." The Cream of Wheat Broadcast. CBS, March 3, 1935. Hamilton College Collection.
"The Town Crier." CBS, November 1936. Houghton Library, Harvard. This program concerned John Gielgud's performance as Hamlet.
"The Town Crier." The Granger Radio Program. CBS, March 9 through July 6, 1937. Hamilton College Collection.
". . . Unto the Least of These." Published in *The Reader's Digest*, XXXIV (May 1939), 89–90.
"Woollcott Speaking. The Battle Hymn of the Republic." For DuPont Cavalcade of America. CBC, December 4, 1940. Hamilton College Collection.

SECONDARY SOURCES

ADAMS, SAMUEL HOPKINS. A. *Woollcott, His Life and His World*. New York: Reynal & Hitchcock, 1945. The earliest Woollcott biography by the famous muckraker, who was also a Hamilton College alumnus and a long-time friend of Woollcott. Attempts to portray both the attractive and the unattractive in Woollcott's character.
———. "Aisle Seats for Mr. Woollcott." *Harper's Magazine*, CXC (January 1945), 154–59. Part 1 of two parts of Woollcott's life from Adams' book on Woollcott; covers early years as *Times* drama critic and the Shubert fight.
———. "Alexander Woollcott, Town Crier." *Harper's Magazine*, CXC (February 1945), 269–79. Part 2 of two parts of Woollcott's life. The trials and successes of "The Town Crier." Explains how Woollcott's sentimentalism caused him to be "conned" by two nonexistent spinsters.

————. "The World of A. Woollcott." *The Reader's Digest*, XLII (May 1943), 9–13. Details some of the things that made Woollcott a living legend.

ATKINSON, BROOKS. *Broadway*. New York: The Macmillan Company, 1970. Excellent overview of Broadway history by one of the critics who succeeded to Woollcott's post on the *Times*. Contains useful sections on Woollcott's stature as a critic and his influence on dramatic criticism.

"Authors Into Actors." *The Saturday Review of Literature*, XXIII (April 5, 1941), 15. Short article on authors turned actors.

BEETLE, DAVID H. "Lavender and Old Torsos, A Report on the Woollcott Library." *Harper's Magazine*, CLXXXVIII (May 1944), 500–501. The kind and variety of Woollcott's books donated to Hamilton College.

BRACKETT, CHARLES. *Entirely Surrounded*. New York: Alfred A. Knopf, 1934. A novel based upon the characters and activities at Woollcott's house on Neshobe Island in Lake Bomoseen, Vermont. Woollcott, Dorothy Parker, Harpo Marx, and other habitués of the island are clearly recognizable in their fictional counterparts.

BROWN, JOHN MASON. "Bellona's Bridegroom." In *Seeing Things*, pp. 300–301. New York, London: Whittlesey House, McGraw-Hill Book Company, Inc., 1946, Discussion of Woollcott's enthusiasm for *What Price Glory?*

————. "Introduction." *The Portable Woollcott*. ed. Joseph Hennessy, pp. xi–xxviii. New York: The Viking Press, 1946. Up to this time, the most complete and perceptive assessment of Woollcott's qualities as a writer; emphasizes all of Woollcott's strengths as a technician. A fusion of Brown's previously published articles in the *Saturday Review of Literature*.

————. "Let Right Be Done." In *Seeing More Things*, pp. 38–39. New York and Toronto: Whittlesey House, McGraw-Hill Book Company, Inc., 1948. Woollcott's defense of the young boy in Britain's famous Archer-Shee case.

————. "The Midas Touch." In *Seeing More Things*, pp. 299–304. New York and Toronto: Whittlesey House, McGraw-Hill Book Company, Inc., 1948. Contains an interesting short anecdote about Woollcott.

————. "Mr. Woollcott Comes for Dinner." In *Broadway in Review*, pp. 88–95. New York: W. W. Norton & Company, 1940. A good defense of Woollcott's writing style. Brown also criticizes Monty Woolley and Chifton Webb in *The Man Who Came to Dinner*.

————. "That Other Alexander." *The Saturday Review of Literature*, XXVIII (June 23, 1945), 28–30. Reprinted in *Seeing Things*. A flamboyant defense of Woollcott's personality and writings with an interesting comparison of Woollcott with Dr. Samuel Johnson. Also a critical review of Adams' *A. Woollcott, His Life and His World*.

_____. "Woollcott in the Flesh—Part I." *The Saturday Review of Literature*. XXIX (March 16, 1946), 38–40, 42. Brown reminiscences about the many sides of the Woollcott personality and tells some new anecdotes.

_____. "Woollcott in Print—Part II." *The Saturday Review of Literature*, XXIX (March 23, 1946), 40–44. A positive article differentiating between Woollcott the critic and Woollcott the writer. Encourages the reader to note the difference.

_____. "Woollcott Speaking." In "Seeing Things," *The Saturday Review of Literature*, XXIX (January 19, 1946), 32–35. Woollcott's letters to George Kaufman.

CASE, FRANK. *Tales of a Wayward Inn: Algonquin.* New York: Garden City Publishing Co., Inc., 1938. Personal account of the "Algonquin Round Table" by the proprietor of the Algonquin Hotel.

CERF, BENNETT. "Trade Winds: The Day Before He Died." *The Saturday Review of Literature*, XXVI (March 13, 1943), 12. Stories about two clever letters Woollcott wrote to two friends the day before he died.

_____. "Woollcott, A Minority Report." *The American Mercury*, LIX (August 1944), 173–79. Article attempts to take the deification out of the Woollcott myth.

_____. "The Woollcott Myth, A Minority Report." In *Try and Stop Me: A Collection of Stories, Mostly Humorous*, pp. 77–87. New York: Simon and Schuster, 1944. This longer article relates Cerf's personal experiences with Woollcott; explains the cause of the rift between them at Random House that caused Cerf to strike Woollcott from the review list.

CONNELLY, MARC. *Voices Off Stage, A Book of Memories.* New York, Chicago, San Francisco: Holt, Rinehart and Winston, 1968. Contains several anecdotes about Woollcott, particularly the one that Connelly calls "the dinner at Frohman's."

DODD, LORING HOLMES. "Town Crier: Alexander Woollcott." In *Celebrities at Our Hearthside*, pp. 71–75. Boston: Dresser, Chapman & Grimes, Inc., Publishers, 1959. Mr. Dodd details the visits of Woollcott to Clark College as lecturer, with Woollcott's comments and his biographical data liberally sprinkled in.

DRENNAN, ROBERT E. *The Algonquin Wits.* New York: The Citadel Press, 1968. A compilation of the best known "wisecracks" of the "Algonquin Wits"; includes a substantial number of Woollcott's.

FORD, COREY. *The Time of Laughter.* Foreword by Frank Sullivan. Boston: Little, Brown and Company, 1967. One of the best-written, most perceptive firsthand accounts of the "Algonquin Wits" and their era (by a younger member of the circle).

"Four Best-Selling Personalities." *The Literary Digest*, CXXI (January 11, 1936), 28. These were considered the best sellers of the time: Woollcott, Sinclair Lewis, T. E. Lawrence, and Anne Lindbergh.

"From London." *Time*, XXXVIII (October 20, 1941), 57–58. Woollcott
broadcasts from London with his usual heart-throbs and human interest
quips.

FULLER, TIMOTHY. "The Story of Jack and Jill As It Might Be Told by
William Faulkner, P. G. Wodehouse, and Alexander Woollcott." *The
Saturday Review of Literature*, XV (December 19, 1936), 10–11. Illus-
trates Woollcott's distinctive style in comparison with Faulkner's and
Wodehouse's.

GIBBS, WOLCOTT. "Big Nemo." In *More in Sorrow* pp. 79–125. New York:
Henry Holt and Company, 1958. A fascinating commentary on all
facets of Woollcott's life—writing, personality, strengths, and
weaknesses. Also has fine, and in some cases new, anecdotes about
Woollcott and his friends and enemies.

GORDON, RUTH. *Myself Among Others*. New York: Atheneum, 1971. A
recent autobiography by a lifelong admirer of Woollcott. An especially
lenient and understanding view of Woollcott's friends and activities.

GRANT, JANE. *Ross, The New Yorker and Me*. New York: Reynal and Com-
pany in Association with William Morrow & Company, Inc., 1968.
Intimate, unflattering account of the personal relationship between
Woollcott and the Harold Rosses.

A *Guide to Archives and Manuscripts in the United States*, ed. Philip M.
Hamer, p. 257. New Haven: Yale University Press, 1961. A list of the
Woollcott papers in Houghton Library at Harvard.

HAMMOND, PERCY. "Alexander Woollcott—Debut." In *The Passionate
Playgoer: A Personal Scrapbook*, ed. George Oppenheimer, pp. 556–
57. New York: The Viking Press, 1958. About Woollcott's debut as an
actor in *Brief Moment*. Contends Woollcott is a good end man.

HACKETT, ALICE. ed. *70 Years of Best Sellers 1895–1965*. New York
and London: R. R. Bowker Company, 1967. Woollcott is listed in
1934–1935 for *While Rome Burns*.

HARRIMAN, MARGARET (CASE). *The Vicious Circle; The Story of the Algonquin Round Table*. New York: Rinehart & Co., Inc., 1951. Most complete, most reliable account of the growth, development, and disinte-
gration of the "Algonquin Wits," by the daughter of Frank Case,
proprietor of the Algonquin.

HOYT, EDWIN PALMER. *Alexander Woollcott: The Man Who Came to Dinner; a biography*. New York: Abelard-Schuman, 1968. Written partly
in reaction against the negative side of the Adams biography. Contains
a good deal of information not in the Adams biography, especially
large amounts of direct quotation.

ISAACS, EDITH J. R. "II. The Theatre of Alexander Woollcott," *Theatre
Arts*, XXVI (March 1942), 191–96. Critical analyses of three major
points that made Woollcott the unchallenged storyteller and critic of
his time. Some Woollcott reactions to certain plays are cited.

KAHN, E. J., JR. *The World of Swope*. New York: Simon and Schuster, 1965. Contains a full and reasonably objective account of Woollcott's close association with the influential executive editor of the *World*.

KEATS, JOHN. *You Might as Well Live. The Life and Times of Dorothy Parker*. New Yorker: Simon and Schuster, 1970. Well-written biography; contains an intimate view of Woollcott's personal relationship with Dorothy Parker, Robert Benchley, Donald Ogden Stewart, and others.

MASON, E. S. "Fourier and Anarchism." *The Quarterly Journal of Economics* XLII (February 1928), 228–62. Mason builds a good case in proving Fourier to be Anarchist rather than Socialist. Useful in understanding the Phalanx.

MARX, HARPO, WITH ROWLAND BARBER. *Harpo Speaks!* New York: Bernard Geis Associates; distributed by Random House, 1961. Bulky account of the life and career of Harpo Marx; contains extensive information upon the long friendship between Marx and Woollcott..

"Mr. Woollcott Is Off the Air." *The Christian Century*, LIII (February 19, 1936), 285. Woollcott's refusal to return to broadcasting because of restrictions on free speech, especially about Hitler and Mussolini.

NACHMAN, GERALD. "Who's Afraid of the Broadway Critics?" *More. The Media Magazine*, VII (July-August 1977), 18–22. Helps place Woollcott in perspective with regard to other American drama critics from Woollcott's time to the present day.

NATHAN, GEORGE JEAN. "Alexander Woollcott, The Seidlitz Powder in Times Square." In *The Magic Mirror. Selected Writings on the Theatre*. Ed., together with an Introduction, Thomas Quinn Curtiss, pp. 64–74. New York: Alfred A. Knopf, 1960. A vitriolic attack upon Woollcott as a young drama critic and especially upon the tone and style of Woollcott's reviews.

NOLAN, PAUL T. *Marc Connelly*. TUSAS 149. New York: Twayne Publishers, Inc., 1969. Contains widely scattered but enlightening references to Woollcott in relation to the theater of his time.

NORTON, ELLIOT. "Puffers, Pundits and Other Play Reviewers. A Short History of American Dramatic Criticism." In *The American Theater: A Sum of Its Parts*, Collection of the distinguished Addresses Prepared Expressly for the Symposium, "The American Theatre—A Cultural Process," at the first American College Theatre Festival, Washington, D.C., 1969, pp. 317–36. New York, Hollywood, London, Toronto: Samuel French, Inc., 1971. History of dramatic criticism, with Norton's chapter leading up to Woollcott from Poe in 1845.

PARKER, DOROTHY. "A Valentine for Mr. Woollcott." In *Vanity Fair. Selections from America's Most Memorable Magazine. A Cavalcade of the 1920's and 1930's*, eds. Cleveland Amory and Frederic Bradlee, pp. 290–91. New York: The Viking Press, Publishers, 1960. Mrs. Parker covers the subject of her friend Woollcott quite completely, honestly, and warmly.

PHILISTINA. *Alec the Great. An Account of the Curious Life and Extraordinary Opinions of the Late Alexander Woollcott.* New York: Avalon Press, 1943. The real name of the author remains unknown, though the name "Philistina" and the gender of the first person narrator indicate that a woman wrote the book. Ostensibly a first person biography, the book portrays Woollcott as being in love with a twelve year old girl. Teichmann (*Smart Aleck*, p. 12) observes that the depiction of this love affair anticipates "Nabokov's masterpiece, *Lolita*, by twenty years." Though "Philistina" provides a vast amount of information that is borne out by the known facts of Woollcott's life, I have not considered the material in this book valid for scholarly purposes. Therefore I have taken no information from it.

PICKETT, CALDER M. "A Paper for the Doughboys: *Stars and Stripes In World War I*," *The Journalism Quarterly*, XLII (Winter 1965), 60–68. A history of the *Stars and Stripes* in World War I. Includes the famous story about Woollcott's *Verdun Belle*.

STAGG, JERRY. *The Brothers Shubert.* New York: Random House, 1968. The Shuberts' constant wars with the various critics including Woollcott.

TARKINGTON, BOOTH. "Ave Atque Vale, A. W.," *The Atlantic Monthly*, CLXXI (June 1943), 64. Very affectionate tribute to Woollcott.

TEICHMANN, HOWARD. "By George S. Kaufman and . . . ," New York *Times Magazine*, November 13, 1966, pp. 64, 67, 69–70, 72, 74, 77, 79–80, 82, 84, 87. Comprehensive article about George S. Kaufman and those with whom he collaborated.

———. *George S. Kaufman: An Intimate Portrait.* New York: Atheneum, 1972. Contains many previously unpublished anecdotes about Woollcott and Kaufman.

———. *Smart Aleck. The wit, world and life of Alexander Woollcott.* New York: William Morrow and Company, Inc., 1976. The most recent Woollcott biography. Largely anecdotal and by far the most readable of the biographies. Contains a good deal of new information.

THURBER, JAMES. *The Years with Ross.* "An Atlantic Monthly Press Book." Boston: Little, Brown and Company, 1959. Account of Woollcott's stormy association with Ross and *The New Yorker* by a member of the staff who admits personal dislike for Woollcott.

WALKER, DANTON. "The Man Who Came to Dinner," *Theatre Arts*, XXXV (January 1951), 31, 96. Written by Woollcott's secretary; this incisive article describes Woollcott's mastery of the language and its literature.

WHITE, E. B. "White House Callers (With Grateful Acknowledgment to the Late Finley Peter Dunne), "*The New Yorker*, XVII (March 15,

1941), 19. Tongue-in-cheek article about Woollcott's and Joe Hennessey's visit to the Franklin Roosevelts.

WILSON, EDMUND. "Alexander Woollcott of the Phalanx." In *Classics and Commercials; A Literary Chronicle of the Forties by Edmund Wilson*, pp. 87–93. New York: Farrar, Straus, 1950. Discusses Woollcott's likes and dislikes on a variety of subjects from reporting to the Classics. Includes a sympathetic obituary that balances hostile ones.

————. "Woollcott and Fourier," *The Nation*, CLVI (February 6, 1943), 194–96. Wilson believes Woollcott's attempts always to be himself regardless of circumstances stem from his early associations at the Phalanx.

WINTERICH, JOHN T. "This Is Woollcott . . . ." *The Saturday Review of Literature*, XI (February 23, 1935), 505. Sprawling article; covers Woollcott's talents from World War I to his debut on Broadway in *Brief Moment*.

————. *Squads Write! A Selection of the Best Things in Prose, Verse and Cartoon from "The Stars and Stripes." Official Newspaper of the A.E.F.*, ed., and with not too serious comment by John T. Winterich, pp. 60-64, 67–68. New York and London: Harper and Brothers Publishers, 1931. Winterich and Woollcott mingle with the doughboys as correspondents for *Stars and Stripes*. Tells the story of how Woollcott insisted that he write the story of Verdun Belle.

Index

The works of Woollcott are listed under his name.
Multiple word headings are alphabetized word-by-word.

818.52
W 913

106937